D1577664

Dangerous Book for Idiots

Published in 2010 by Prion
An imprint of the Carlton Publishing Group
20 Mortimer Street
London W1T 3JW

Copyright © 2010 Carlton Books Limited

A CIP catalogue record for this book is available from the British
Library.

ISBN 978 1 85375 791 4

Printed in the UK by CPI Mackays, Chatham, ME5 8TD

10 9 8 7 6 5 4 3 2 1

Chaz Nuffington-Twattt's

Dangerous
Book
for
Idiots

PRION

Warning

Please don't really try any of the stunts and ideas in this book.

This book is intended for amusement only and is not to be taken as a guide or to offer genuine advice or taken seriously. Many of the instructions are dangerous, illegal and represent a real threat to life. Neither the author nor the publisher accepts responsibility for any accident, injury, loss or damage (including any consequential loss) that a reader may suffer after using the ideas, information, procedures or advice offered in this book.

YOU HAVE BEEN WARNED!

Abnormally Dangerous Activity – A definition

An undertaking so dangerous that, even if precautions and reasonable care are used, cannot be safely performed and anyone who engages in it is strictly liable for any resulting injuries and damage, especially if...

1. there is a risk of serious harm to people or property.
2. the activity cannot be performed in some other way that avoids those risks.
3. the undertaking does not normally occur at the location where it is to take place.

So now you know!

Contents

Introduction

Are you stark raving bonkers? Have you no care for life and limb? Too much adrenaline and not enough brain cells? Do you like hospital food? Then this is just the book for you. A collection of no-brainer misadventures, pranks, sports and dare-devil high jinks that no-one in their right mind would even contemplate trying.

There's a treacherous world out there just waiting for someone like you – with guts, a lust for adventure and absolutely no sense whatsoever. So, make sure you've got the address of your local hospital handy, write your last will and testament and get ready to roll with these 100 death-defying ideas...

And, at the end of each crazy idea, because you're such an idiot – we'll tell you your chances of getting arrested, dying or, at the very least, incurring serious injury.

Enjoy yourself, and don't get hurt!

Chaz Nuffington-Twattt,
Ward 10, St Dick's College Hospital, Cheshunt

Part One

It's Not Going to Kill You

We thought we'd start you off on some soft options. Dangerous pursuits for those who still like to sleep with their teddy bears. This is not to say you wouldn't get hurt pretty badly but you need something to get the adrenaline going. Anyway, you'll be able to laugh about it – once the bandages come off...

Walking on Red Hot Coals

Mind over matter? Supernatural powers? Or just plain dangerous fun?

It's practised by countless tribes and religions, stoned-out-of-their-brains hippies and middle managers on teamwork exercises, so surely your average idiot can stumble barefoot over 15 ft (4.5m) of glowing coals without ending up in intensive care?

Your naked size tens will be slapping down on coals that measure from 1,000 – 1,500 °F (550 – 820 °C) – think of that burger sizzling as it's placed on the barbeque. So you'd think that there's a reasonable chance you're going to get your tootsies singed. Actually, the activity should be pretty harmless – the science of heat transfer means you have a short contact time before the coals raise your skin temperature to burning point. Move on at the right pace and you'll be fine – in theory.

How come so many people come through unscathed and yet you, dear idiot, will collect third-degree burns? Because you lack any real faith? Because your self-belief falters at the crucial moment? No, simply because you can't be bothered to learn a few basic safety hints like just walking on coals and not timber or metal. Let a layer of ash settle first, walk briskly and don't show off by catwalking, moonwalking or stopping to wave.

Dangerous Idiot Odds
Arrest 0
Injury 4
Death 1

Get ready to bare your soles as you display your flaming feet of fortitude

Penis Weight Hanging

If size really does matter are you man enough to do something about it?

Worried about a lack of inches? Don't go answering those pumps and pill-pushing emails. The source of your angst has dogged men across the world since time immemorial and the possible solution is as just as ancient – even practiced, they say, by the ancient Egyptians. This is weight training unlike any you'll find at your local gym...

The technique is to *carefully* – pay attention to that word, idiots – stretch the tissues of your Johnson by strapping weights to the organ and letting gravity do its stuff. Create a small sock for your todger, reasonably tight fitting but not enough to cut off your circulation. Sew on loops either side of the sock, thread some string through and attach your weights. Start off with 5 lbs (2 kg) and work your way up towards 15 lbs (7 kg), week by week. If you do this every day for an hour or so, you could see some results.

Sounds great doesn't it? If you are happy sitting watching the match as your wedding tackle works out, you could be walking tall with an extra inch or so. Of course, there are dangers – it's your dearest and most sensitive organ we're talking about here. We could start with chronic pain, scarring or impotence – crossing your legs yet? Or, if your hanging device does stop the circulation, you could end up with gangrene and have to have the whole thing amputated.

Dangerous Idiot Odds
Arrest 0 (as long as you do it in private)
Injury 3
Death 0

If God wanted you to hang things off it he'd have given you a hook

Lighting Your Farts

Go on! You know you've always wanted to light one up, even if it's just out of curiosity...

Are you carrying around a human blow-torch or just a flickering candle? Putting a flame to your bottom breeze is the ultimate test of your fart power. Quite simply the more gas you are expelling, the more impressive the explosion.

Everyone's farts contain a mixture of gases, including the highly flammable hydrogen sulphide, methane and hydrogen, and when exposed to a naked flame – a match or a lighter – they'll ignite. The size of your fart and the precise make-up of these gases will determine the nature of the pyroflatulence.

People often call it "Blueflaming" as the methane and carbon dioxide produce a blue hue, but if you look carefully on the video your mate has no doubt made, you'll also see some yellow (from the sodium), purple (from the potassium) and even green (from copper).

The whole show is most impressive when performed in the dark due to the often impromptu nature of the display and possible burns. With your lighter at the ready, sit down and just rock backwards to rest on the small of your back. Pass you lighter arm under the back of your thighs, a few inches from your butt and light up in good time. All being well, you'll really rip the light fantastic – if not, you could have trouble sitting down for a while...

Dangerous Idiot Odds
Arrest 2
Injury 3
Death 0

Is it this skill that truly separates man from the apes?

Extreme Mosh Pit Action

Strictly Come Dancing – for the lunatic fringe...

"That's not dangerous. It's just some punk-thrash-death-metal rock band and a load of scruffy kids in denim dancing." You reckon? The mosh-pit can be the scene of intense legal arbitrary violence – an arena ideally suited to the idiot for whom bodily injury holds no fear.

Moshing or slamming is the practice of pushing, bouncing, and slamming off of other people to the music of a live performance. People don't go moshing to deliberately hurt others – and usually help pick up the fallen – but in the adrenaline-fuelled, flailing of heads, arms and legs, injuries are inevitable.

In the pit, anything goes – punching, kicking, biting – but, like any dance, moshing has its own moves: *The Bodyslam* is performed in mid-air by slamming your upper body against a fellow mosher; *The Cyclone* finds two dancers joining hands and spinning uncontrollable regardless of who is in the way; and *Thrashing* requires jumping and flinging your arms and legs without any care or attention.

At the zenith of mosh pit action are the stage dive and crowd surf; climbing onto the stage and launching yourself into the slamming hordes in the hope they will catch you. Having landed, you can then be tossed around in the air by the mass of arms until someone tires of it and lets you fall unceremoniously to the ground.

Dangerous Idiot Odds
Arrest 1
Injury 4
Death 1

Could be the only time you'll get an apology for a punch in the face

Beer Enema

Getting drunk from the bottom up

We all know that feeling – you just can't take another drink but you're not quite drunk enough. Or maybe, you know you just can't go home stinking of beer yet again. The beer enema is the perfect solution for every sad alcoholic idiot around...

Before you start, be aware that alcohol is absorbed much more quickly in the intestines than in the stomach – you are going to get drunk that much quicker than drinking it – so absorb anything stronger than beer and you could be looking at some serious damage.

Your rectal imbibing can be done in the traditional surgical way with towels, funnels and a length of piping or you can just do it right there in the bar room. Lubricate a bottle of beer and insert it where the sun don't shine and bend over to pour the booze directly up the alley.

The beer is going direct to your blood stream – not passing the liver and not collecting £200 – so no toxins are being filtered and you are going to get a pretty sudden and intense intoxication. Doing one bottle of beer in an enema over three minutes is pretty much equivalent to drinking 20 bottles in an hour.

Police Spray on

Dangerous Idiot Odds	
Arrest	2
Injury	2
Death	1

If it's a pain in the butt – you need to take more care...

Your Burger

For those who like their food a little spicy...

So you like hot sauce on your food? A spicy ketchup or a dash of tabasco maybe? You're doing well – that's a rating of 50,000 on the Scoville scale, the scientific means of measuring the heat of chillies. Considering the Jalapeno is a mere 8,000, you're already a fair bit up the scale. Ready for the naga jolokia chilli? At around one million on the scale it is smeared on fences and used in smoke bombs as a safety precaution against wild elephants. If you're going to touch it, wear gloves. Ok, you sweat a lot and maybe need an extra beer to cool down but you can take it. Can it get any more macho than this? Yes.

 The US police pepper spray is made of chilli powder and is five times as hot as the naga, coming in at five million on the Scoville register. When sprayed in the faces of demonstrators, violent criminals or someone who gives the cops a funny look, it can cause a blindness which lasts from 15-30 minutes, a burning sensation of the skin for an hour and uncontrollable coughing. On the plus side, it comes in a really handy spray dispenser that can fit in the pocket or your handbag. Ideal for spicing up that late night kebab...

Dangerous Idiot Odds
Arrest 2
Injury 3
Death 0

Some like it hot, others like it hotter, you like it hottest

Ice Hole Swimming

Introduce your body to a little shock treatment...

The water's cold. Not that holiday sea cold, when you have to run in and get under water as quick as possible, but freezing cold. Your body tenses with shock, your blood rushes to the heart, you gasp for air and your teeth start to chatter...

Welcome to *Avantouinti*, a pastime practiced by over 100,000 people in Finland. There, cutting a hole in the ice and submerging yourself in the water is considered good for the health even helping to cure or prevent depression – despite the fact that the rush they feel is through experiencing borderline hypothermia.

Tempted, though you undoubtedly will be, to perform your best bomb – it is advised that you lower yourself in gently, taking deep breaths and keeping your head well above the water. If you survive the possible heart attack, don't be tempted to show off and stay in for more than a minute or you'll cross that borderline into actual hypothermia.

It's probably worth leaving not just your skimpy towel by the "pool" but a whole set of warm clothes, for climbing out of the water in sub-zero conditions presents more problems. If your hair is wet it could freeze and start rapidly reducing your body temperature, your trunks could freeze to your body (at the most painful place possible!) and if you warm up too quickly, the shock to the body can be fatal.

Dangerous Idiot Odds
Arrest 0
Injury 3
Death 1

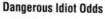

And you thought the local swimming pool was a little chilly!

Wasabi Snorting

Need to clear those sinuses? This will help...

If you are a fan of Johnny Knoxville and his madcap *Jackass* stunts you might remember this dare and – as they say – the hilarious consequences. But can the humble idiot, with no Hollywood contract or slightest hope of stardom, ever replicate such a feat?

Wasabi is the green horseradish that accompanies the Japanese food, sushi. Just a tiny dot can provide a chilli-type heat rush and a sharp flavour that can clear your sinuses in seconds. It's mad enough to try to eat more than the smallest coin-sized dollop of paste – but you'd need to be a real idiot to snort the stuff. Over to you...

Wasabi powder is added to water to make the paste and has the same tear-inducing, instantaneous nasal passage-clearing and nerve-chiming qualities of the root. Make a line of powder 1-2 in (2.5-5 cm), no more – then take a rolled up bank note and insert the end up one nostril. Block your other nostril and sniff in deeply, drawing the wasabi up your nose in one go. It will be agony for a minute or so, the pain reaching right up into your brain, but you'll be able to speak and stand up straight again after 15 minutes or so. You'll probably never eat sushi again though.

Dangerous Idiot Odds

Arrest 0

Injury 1

Death 0

Who is that jumping around the kitchen clutching his nose? Oh...

Grow a Bee Beard

A challenge with a sting in the tail...

Still unable to grow any impressive facial hair? Fear not, the bee beard is a simple application of 20,000 or more bees on your face that will give you not only an intellectual look, but will also move and buzz in the creepiest way imaginable. And all you risk is a sting or two (thousand) and some odd looks from strangers.

To get the bees on your face, you need to hang the queen from a cage – fix it just below your chin for an impressive goatee appearance. Then, swab your face and neck with queen pheromones (available from online bee-keeping sites). The swarm of bees belonging to the queen will be attracted to the cage, resulting in a swarm that is affixed to your face.

Two things to remember – don't panic or swat, this will just infuriate the little stingers, and keep your mouth shut. At first you will feel the beard tickle as the bees crawl over your face, then it will feel warm and finally you'll feel like you are wearing a prickly, humming scarf that is moving around your face.

Now you've done the easy part, it's time for the full beard effect. Strip off and daub the pheremones over your naked body.

Dangerous Idiot Odds	
Arrest	1
Injury	3
Death	1

The world record was set by Mark Biancaniello in California with a 350,000 full body Italian bee beard. However, he used Italian bees, a particularly docile breed. It would be unbecoming of any real idiot not to use the Africanized "Killer Bee" (see page 31).

You said you wanted something to leave you buzzing with excitement…

Competitive Nettle Eating

For those who need to be stung into action...

Eating handfuls of stinging nettles as a competitive sport first came to the fore at the Bottle Inn in the tiny Dorset village of Marshwood, population 300, around 1986 when two farmers settled an argument as to who had the longest nettles on their land. Now hundreds of competitors descend on the village to face an hour of munching their way through the leaves.

The rules are strict. Only fresh, raw nettles provided can be eaten, no mouth-numbing substances are allowed and the nettles must be swallowed and kept down. The winner is whoever finishes with the most 2 ft (60 cm) stalks, stripped of their leaves. Those looking to triumph will need to munch their way through nearly 50 ft (15 m) of nettles with only a few pints of ale to wash it down.

The leaves don't taste too bad, being described as resembling spinach, but they can pack a painful sting. The real art to the "sport" is to fold the leaves carefully, enclosing the stinging edges well inside the resulting package. Saliva can prevent the stinging, so the mouth needs to be kept moist, but any dry areas of the mouth will be stung. Competitors receive many stings around the mouth and often find their tongues turning black and lips swelling.

Dangerous Idiot Odds
Arrest 0
Injury 3
Death 0

It'll count as part of your five-a-day

Dustbin Baseball

Wake the neighbours with the game that's sweeping the suburbs...

While many of the pursuits outlined in this book require specialist equipment, skills, animals or even practise, I feel it's important to include some activities that can be undertaken around the home with the minimum of preparation. All this particular game needs is a metal dustbin, a baseball bat and two bored idiots.

Empty the bin of any rubbish and make sure there's no rotting residue still clinging to the bottom. On second thoughts, don't check – it'll add a little spice to an already pointless exercise. Now put the bin over your head and prepare to let the game begin. While you have been doing this your mate will have been watching with a smirk and can get ready to strike.

The first rule of Dustbin Baseball is there are no rules. Your mate can aim for any part of the bin and doesn't have to give you any warning. You may wish to keep various body parts from contact with the bin but you should be perfectly safe, depending on the quality of your bin. Although your ear drums can get a right battering.

Dangerous Idiot Odds
Arrest 1
Injury 2
Death 0
Stupidity 5

When he gets tired of hitting you, get him to swap positions… good luck with that

Bubble Wrapping Sea Suit

Don't think of going on the water without one...

Looking for a buoyancy aid that will enable you to float around at sea, however choppy it gets? No. Me neither. But make yourself a bubble wrapping sea suit and you'll be the envy of any other seafaring idiots out there.

Bubble wrapping, the padded transparent plastic packing material, as you will know if you are one of those irritating people who are obsessed with bursting the little pouches, are full of small, sealed air pockets. Make yourself a suit out of enough of the wrapping or just wrap yourself in it and you'll find it perfect for keeping you buoyant in the ocean.

There are just a couple of small drawbacks. You'll need plenty of the stuff – around 60 ft (18 m) or so, to make sure you keep afloat – and being wrapped tightly in so much material will mean your mobility is limited. You might just be able to walk across the beach but once in the sea you'll be at the mercy of the tide and currents. And, of course, you'll look a complete idiot.

Dangerous Idiot Odds	
Arrest	1
Injury	2
Death	1

Dangerous, useless and unstylish – it's the perfect accessory for the sea-going idiot

Human Bowling

A supreme-ish test of body co-ordination, accuracy and sheer stupidity.

You'll like this. It's a little like ten-pin bowling, but you won't need those stinking shoes, your own ball or a disgustingly coloured baggy shirt – and you won't be bowling against some jerk who has nothing better to do than spend every night on the alley. Nope. This is just you against the skittles...

First, you need to collect a load of large cardboard boxes from your local supermarket (perhaps the one you've been banned from after Supermarket Joust – see page 73). You'll need at least ten and maybe some in reserve. Now choose your skittle alley, it can be indoors or out but should be at least 33 ft (10 m) long.

Take your ten boxes and build a pyramid at the end of your space, placing four at the bottom, three on the second row, two on the third and the last box on top. Now measure 10 ft (3 m) from the boxes and mark you jump line.

You must start your run up from the end of the space, reach the jump line and launch yourself at the pyramid. Any of the boxes that fall are removed and you return to the start line and start again – this time trying to fell the remaining boxes.

The sport is still in its infancy but future editions of this book will try to deal with developing techniques and strategies.

Dangerous Idiot Odds
Arrest 0
Injury 3
Death 0

What works for you? A spread-eagle flight, the spinning leap or the kamikaze crash?

The Multi-Storey Downhill

It's what the office chair was made for...

Every day, up and down the country, at around four in the afternoon, there are bored, dangerous idiots desperately seeking ways to pass the time until they knock off for the day. Few of them will go through their working lives without having a race along the corridors on their office chairs, but fewer, if any, will consider taking the sport to its logical conclusion...

The multi-storey car park provides a ready-made ideal course for a real office chair downhill challenge. A race from the top to the bottom of a town centre car park will provide enough short downhill stretches to build up some serious speed, some difficult turns to test the riders, control and real danger in the chances of meeting a proper vehicle head-on during the race.

There are a number of riding positions open to the racer, such as "At My Desk" – sitting normally, face front with your legs just off the ground but close enough for control or "The Christine Keeler" – sitting reverse on the chair with your legs astride the back of the chair. Whichever position you adopt, you are almost certain to come off at some time and considering you'll reach speeds of up to 10 mph (16 kph), it's worth putting some padding and a lid on.

Dangerous Idiot Odds
Arrest 2
Injury 3
Death 1

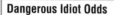

Double the danger if the boss catches you...

Dangerous Gardening

It's a death-trap out in the garden...

Is it possible to make gardening a dangerous activity? A reckless attitude with the strimmer may lead to some blood on the fuchsias, but otherwise, chronic bad back pain is the worst you are going to face. Unless, that is, you follow the idiots' guide to dangerous gardening and start growing a few plants you won't hear mentioned on *Gardener's World*...

Your garden will, of course, have some well-developed stinging nettles but you might also consider a bush such as the African sumac, which, if touched, causes a blisters and rashes; a perennial like the giant hogweed (get its sap on your skin in sunlight and it'll cause severe burns); or consider growing poison ivy with its rash-inducing oil, urushiol.

For depth and perspective in your design you might like *the stinging tree* from Australia. Even if you wear gloves, the leaves will leave tiny hairs in your hands that give intense pain. You can even get nose bleeds from the hairs blowing in the air. Perhaps you might also develop a manchineel tree from the Caribbean – this gift of nature can spit caustic sap at you when cut.

And, of course, there are cacti – the beautiful jumping cholla is the pick of these prickly devils. Its spines can penetrate shoe leather. Try to pull them out and they'll rip your skin off.

When you see that sweet old man pottering in the garden,
think again – he could be one of us...

Home-Made Fireworks

If you want one mother of an explosion – make it yourself.

This is how firework night ends, not with a bang but a whimper... Sick of feeble firecrackers, wretched rockets and the dreadful anti-climax of the safety box of fireworks purchased from your local newsagents? Isn't it time you took your life in your hands and woke up the neighbours with some DIY pyrotechnics?

It'll mean risking the odd explosion in the kitchen – and perhaps losing the odd limb – while you get the recipe right. Extract powder from safety fireworks, mix fertilizer and sugar or, if you can, buy some flash or black powder from the local supermarket and add some colour to your mixture (aluminium for white light, strontium salt for red, copper salts for blue, etc.). Now fill a film canister, tennis ball or cardboard tube with your mixture and set about making a fuse package with a hundred or so match heads and a string coated lightly with your explosive mixture.

There's a fair chance you'll be arrested (hopefully not for terrorist activities), suffer third-degree burns, end up minus an eye or a hand and maybe have injured your friends– but you just might have created a pyrotechnic spectacle to remember – now wouldn't that be worth it?

Dangerous Idiot Odds
Arrest 5
Injury 4
Death 2

Too risky? Since when has that put the true idiot off anything?

Part Two
Now, This Could Hurt –
Quite A Lot

Are you the kind to shy away from second-degree burns, multiple stitches and police custody? If so, the next set of stunts might be worth keeping well clear of. We're moving the stupidity level up a few notches and the pain barrier up to severe...

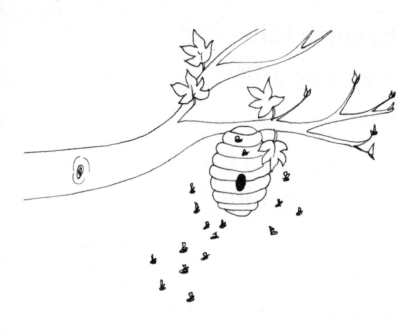

Keeping Killer Bees

Imagine having, at the bottom of the garden, a hive of the most dangerous, savage bees known to man...

In the movie *The Swarm*, great clouds of angry bees attack entire cities and sting hundreds of people to death. Of course, this is pure fiction, but it is the recent rise of the Africanized "Killer Bee" that has given rise to such stories...

The cross-breeding of accidentally released African bees and the ordinary American bee has produced a hybrid, called an Africanized bee – an aggressive, easily agitated and all-round bad boy bee – often referred to as the Killer Bee.

As their keeper it's worth finding out what drives them bonkers. Africanized bees are said to react to disturbance around the hive as well as loud or high-pitched noises (best keep whistling to a minimum), strong odours or fragrances, shiny jewellery and dark clothes. Once angered, they take days to calm down.

These bees love to swarm and, when one bee stings, it releases an alarm smell that causes its mates to become agitated and look for someone to sting too. If you are in the path of a swarm of Africanized bees, you have a 75 percent chance of being attacked. However, it will probably take over 1,000 stings to kill the average person – only two people a year are estimated to die from Killer Bee attacks.

Dangerous Idiot Odds
Arrest 1
Injury 3
Death 1

Not a lot of honey and not much wax but plenty of Bad Attitude Bee

The Most Dangerous Drink in the World

Make mine a double.

Any old fool can get drunk. A devastating cocktail, a few slammers or 14 pints (8 l) of Scruttocks Old Original will do the trick. But how many of us can take a really dangerous drink, a beverage with enough punch to have you seeing flying elephants before you've even opened your packet of pork scratchings?

Perhaps you could start the night with the most notorious of strong liquors, the Green Fairy, i.e. absinthe, with its psychoactive chemical thujone renowned for bringing on hallucinations. Though banned in the US and parts of Europe for much of the 20th century, it is now freely available. Then move onto the Japanese tipple, Habu Saki, a strong rice wine with an interesting addition of a poisonous habu snake whose toxins flavour the drink. It's said that three consecutive shots can stop your heart.

Still standing? Then it's time for a quick shot of *Poitín* (Potcheen), which for centuries has been privately and often illegally distilled from malted barley grain or potatoes in rural Ireland. Extraordinarily alcoholic, it can, if poorly produced, also contain dangerous amounts of methanol and blind or kill.

But enough of the soft drinks, as the night moves on you'll want to move on to the big hitters, the grain alcohols. Get down that bottle of American Everclear, at 190 percent it's strong enough to start your car. They say you should only drink it with a mixer – presumably not the equally strong Polish rectified spirit Spirytus Rektyfikowanya, a drink that is also used as a cleaning solvent. Not that you're going be in any state for housework...

Dangerous Idiot Odds
Arrest 5
Injury 4
Death 2

Dangerous, stupid, needs no skill – and you can do it sitting down watching the match

Sub-Zero Naturism

Get down to your birthday suit and up to the Arctic Circle for a spot of top-notch idiot daring...

A winter's Friday night in the city centre and you're looking tough in just your shirt sleeves. Come Saturday afternoon you are ready to whip your footie shirt off for a quick chant or two and a chance to get on the TV cameras. But are you cut out for the real cold? Welcome to extreme naturism...

The benefits of nudism are manifold – a chance to get out of those stuffy clothes. Let whatever you've got swing naturally and enjoy everything nature's got to give. But where's the fun in playing volleyball in a Dorset campsite when you can do it the idiot's way – in the ice cold. In sub-zero temperatures when you're completely starkers?

How difficult can it be? A few goosepimples and some teeth chattering? The Inuit of the Arctic sometimes go nude in their igloos and naturist hotels in Austrian mountains recommend a roll in the snow after a sauna.

Well for a start *congelatio* is not something you'll enjoy. Frostbite, as ordinary folk call it, can happen to any bits exposed to temperatures below freezing – and you could lose the fingers, toes, nose, ears or – ouch! – your todger. Then there's chilblains, trench foot and hypothermia to worry about – not to mention the obvious loss of self-esteem – so watch out for that wind chill!

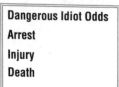

Dangerous Idiot Odds
Arrest
Injury
Death

Intense discomfort, potential loss of limb and humiliation – what's not to like?

Squirting Milk Through Your Eyes

Ahh! He's crying.... oh, no it's, it's euuhhh!

In 2009, in Nanjing city in China, Zhang Yinming drank milk through his nose and then squirted it up to 6 ft (2 m) out of his eyes. It is a truly fantastic, appalling stunt – if you can do it. It's a brilliant enough trick to be able to cry milk tears but if you can actually manage to squirt it from your eyes, you'll be a 100 percent, bona-fide freak act.

The action itself is pretty simple – just swallow some milk and force it up through the nasal passages that connect your throat, nose and eyes. You might have already performed half the trick when you've taken a mouthful of liquid and unexpectedly laughed only to find the liquid coming out of your nose. All you've now got to do is get the milk to go that extra few inches to your tear ducts.

You can do it by squeezing your nose so it can't escape that way or use the Zhang Yinming method and actually snort it up into your nose. Hold your breath and blow as hard as possible.

After a little practice you could have a home horror show— or burst blood vessels, sinus infection and damaged nasal passages...

Dangerous Idiot Odds
Arrest 0
Injury 2
Death 0

You can milk this one for all its worth

Keep a Cassowary

Who's a pretty boy then? Not this brute for sure!

People love a feathered friend – a budgie, parrot or even a cockatoo makes an entertaining companion. If they're over 75 that is. Anyone else with the slightest sense of danger would look to keep something a little less predictable – like a cassowary...

Cassowarys are the world's most dangerous birds – think of a psychotic emu with an anger-management problem. Hailing from the rainforests of Australia and New Guinea, these shy animals have a bony crest on their heads capable of knocking down small trees, and dagger-like sharp claws including a 5 in (12 cm) long middle claw. Growing up to 6 ft (1.8 m) tall and weighing in at over 130lbs (60 kg), it can still reach speeds of 30mph (48 kph) – and in what would be an admirable martial arts move, it is capable of kicking with both legs at the same time.

Many zoos refuse to keep them after injuries to keepers. The cassowary thinks nothing of gutting dogs, killing horses, maiming humans and one even killed a 16-year-old boy by slashing his jugular. Professionals recommend you approach them with cricket pads, a police riot shield and a large beater. So getting it into your back garden could be a real problem – on the other hand, it'll be great to see the look on the cat's face!

Dangerous Idiot Odds	
Arrest	5
Injury	5
Death	2

Always wanted a pet dinosaur? These modern-day equivalents are the nearest you'll get

Fun with a Microwave

If it's too hot in the kitchen... take it outside.

When we were young we'd have to make our own entertainment. Our favourite pastime was seeing what we could explode in the microwave. It didn't go down well with my parents, but it made me the guy I am today.

A bar of soap was brilliant as it mutated into an enormous alien-type splodge; halved grapes light up and dance; a CD or a folded piece of tin foil made for a great light show; and a lighted match stuck in a tea-light gave you your own indoor firework show with a great exploding finale.

The best fun, however, was with a simple egg. Now, everyone knows an egg will explode if microwaved for over 30 seconds – but the art was getting it out of the oven and onto the table to watch it explode in the comfort of your kitchen.

Now I'm older, and after several trips to the burns unit, I searched out a stunt more suited to the mature, dangerous idiot. Step forward the humble can of baked beans. All you need to do is get an extension lead long enough to set the oven in a space clear of the house, place the unopened can in the microwave and on the highest setting, turn on for five minutes. Then leg it...

You should achieve an explosion violent enough to blow the doors off or blow the whole oven into smithereens. However, be careful to leave the beans a minute or so before eating.

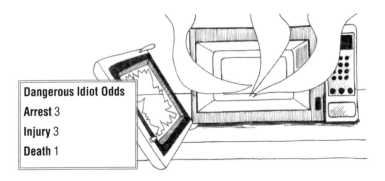

| Dangerous Idiot Odds |
| Arrest 3 |
| Injury 3 |
| Death 1 |

When the going gets tough, the tough get cooking....

Treadmill Terror

Hit the gym for some calorie-burning idiocy.

There's no getting round it, going to the gym gets pretty boring. And there's nothing more soul-destroying than the treadmill, i.e. running on the spot for 10 minutes to find you've worked off the equivalent of two grapes. What everyone is waiting for is someone to entertain them with some ridiculous attempts to hurt himself. And, of course, that someone is you...

Here are a few challenges to see how badly you can hurt yourself – and remember, no touching those side rails.

Hopping: the record for the longest time to hop on one leg on a treadmill at a constant speed of 4 mph (6.5 kph) is 2 min 17 sec and was set by Nicolas Thomas (France) on 23 May 2002.

Running Backwards: supposedly good for your quad and postural muscles – not so great for the back of your head.

Speed Challenge: stand with your legs on each side of the treadmill, hold the side rails and set the speed as fast as you dare. Jump on and prepare to be swept across the room ...

Skateboard Suicide: you'll need to hang on at first for this one... Take your skateboard onto the belt and slowly increase the speed when you are ready. Now it's time for your kickflip!

Dangerous Idiot Odds

Arrest 1 (But you might get banned from the gym)

Injury 3

Death 0

Did you feel the burn? The carpet burn that is

Blindfold Lorry Limbo

How low can you go?

Roller skating under stationary cars while blindfolded has become the latest craze in India, with daredevil skaters flattening their bodies until they are less than 8 in (20 cm) off the ground. To get under the car and out the other side you must be able to maintain a reasonable speed while doing the splits and keeping your head as low as possible. Now an organized competition in the sub-continent, some skaters manage to sail under three cars – and as many as 80 cars – without a blindfold.

And they're under eight years old.

Obviously a child has the advantage of a supple body and a low centre of gravity so it would be unfair to expect a couch potato like you to get down and dirty. However, a similar blindfolded limbo under a stationary lorry – with a clearance of 2-3 ft (60-90 cm) foot – should be possible or give everyone a good laugh.

The kids' technique is worth noting: build up a head of speed and when you think you are approaching the vehicle, gradually let you legs drift apart until you are doing the splits with you feet stretched perpendicular to your legs. Touch your toes and lower your head until your chin can just brush the ground and keep rolling until you sense you have emerged on the other side.

Dangerous Idiot Odds
Arrest 2
Injury 3
Death 1

20 seconds of eye-watering, forehead-smashing, chin-grazing fun

The Ottery St Mary Tar Barrels

A fine tradition passed down through generations of dangerous idiots.

Every year on 5th November, thousands flock to the town of Ottery St Mary in Devon to watch as flaming barrels are carried through the streets. Seventeen burning barrels are carried as, throughout the evening, the size of the adult barrels grow – until a 65lb (30 kg) cask is carried at midnight.

The barrels are filled with straw and paper and the insides are soaked with tar for weeks on end. They are lit outside each of the town's pubs in turn and, once the flames are licking from the barrels, they are hoisted up onto the backs and shoulders of volunteers. The bearers compete with one another to carry the flaming barrels as far as they can before the casks either get too hot to handle or disintegrate in a burning heap in the street. The idea is to carry them as close to the town bonfire as possible.

The explanation for such a bizarre tradition is that the fire pouring from the burning tar barrels originates from a pagan ceremony to cleanse the streets of evil spirits. In most cases, generations of the same family carry the barrels every year and they jealously guard their right to be "rollers" so it might not be possible to join in. However, surely you know a town whose streets are running with evil spirits? Couldn't they do with a little purging from an idiot with a flaming barrel on his back?

Dangerous Idiot Odds	
Arrest	4
Injury	4
Death	1

They call it a quaint tradition; they'll call you a flaming loon

Make a Dry Ice Bomb

A school experiment or a dangerous idiot's stunt?

It's a regular science class experiment, so how dangerous can this be? Conducted by a sensible teacher it is a relatively safe experience, but we're mixing dry ice, high pressure and reckless idiots – so that's ice burns, premature explosions in your face and damage to family members. That's why dry ice bombs are illegal in many states and countries around the world...

Dry ice is solid carbon dioxide. When it reaches a temperature of over –108°F (–78°C) it doesn't melt but turns straight into a vapour – causing the kind of foggy effect you see at rock concerts and theatres. The ice warms up incredibly quickly and expands by a factor of 750. At this point, the smart kids are beginning to guess what's going to happen, the rest of you can wait for the next paragraph.

Take a 4 pint (2l) plastic lemonade bottle and fill it about a quarter full of warm water, add some dry ice and screw the top back on tightly. As the ice turns to vapour the pressure begins to mount inside the bottle. As the bottles are pretty tough you get a lot of pressure building up – it can take anything from 20 seconds to 30 minutes – before the ultimate explosion. For a real treat try taking the bottle outside and putting it under an upturned garbage can – see if you can send your rubbish into space!

Dangerous Idiot Odds
Arrest 4
Injury 3
Death 1

"Exploding soda bottles Batman!" "Remember, idiots are people too, Robin!"

Shave with a Knife

The best a man can get?

No real man is really worthy of the name until he has shaved with a knife. In no way is it an essential skill – you are unlikely to be called for a job interview while camping deep in the jungle without a razor – but it is ridiculous, tricky and dangerous, and that is exactly why you'll soon be sharpening up the bread knife.

The only trick is to have a really sharp knife – such as a hunter's skinning knife – with as thin a blade as possible. Lather your face with a thin film of soap and hold the blade as flat to the surface as you can. Now run the blade smoothly across your beard or stubble, skimming, even scraping but not slicing. Avoid putting any downward pressure on the knife and watch carefully, just in case you are cutting a flap in your face.

Once, twice or more during the shave you are sure to cut yourself, but most cuts should be clean and shallow – you shouldn't bleed too much and they'll heal in a day or two. The difficult areas are the loose skin around the ears and the uneven contours of the chin, and watch out for any unexpected jolts or spasms when you get to the throat area – that could be very messy.

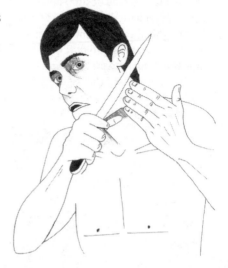

Dangerous Idiot Odds
Arrest 0
Injury 3
Death 1

You're ugly enough already – what's another scar or two?

Fly Like A Bird

Make wings, wear wings, fly!

We can't run fast enough to take off. Muscles would need to protrude 3 ft (90 cm) out of our chests and shoulders. And the aerodynamics of the human body are just not suited to flight. Really? Some people are just so negative...

In events such as Britain's Birdman or the Flugtag that has taken place in Vienna, Florida and Portland, Oregon, successful winged idiots have managed to throw themselves off a pier and fly for getting on for 330 ft (100 m). Considering the Wright Brothers first flight reached only 120 ft (37 m), I'd say these early birdmen have made considerable progress.

All this is not to say that you can just take a running leap off the end of the pier. That's called "jumping in the water" and is an entirely different event. You will need to spend time developing a fast short sprint, building strong upper body muscles and making some wings.

Depending on your knowledge of aerodynamics, your available budget and how much you can be bothered, your wings can be made to any design. Make them as light as possible – use coat hanger wire and bamboo to make a structure and then add bird feathers, thin bedsheets or plastic sheeting. You'll need a wingspan of at least 16 ft (5 m) and, of course, be able to strap or tape the thing on your back and your arms. Happy flying!

The laws of physics? Pah! We spit on their lily-livered spirit

Ride the Wall of Death

They don't make danger like this any more...

The thrills and sometimes spills of this gravity-defying fairground show entertained millions in its heyday in the first half of the 20th century. Now, although reduced to a handful of performers around the world, the Wall of Death is as exciting, risky and scary as ever.

The Wall of Death is a wooden cylinder, like a barrel cut in half, which is around 16 ft (5 m) high and about 30 ft (9 m) in diameter. Motorcyclists, having achieved the required speed to harness the centrifugal force to keep them upright, approach the wall on a ramp and proceed to perform tricks and stunts while riding horizontal to the ground. Spectators stand on a platform around the circumference to watch the show inside the cylinder.

The performance demands courage, balance and the ability to judge your speed –around 60 mph (96 kph) – with absolute precision; try to climb up when you're going too slow or too fast, and you'll immediately fall off. Once you are riding in a horizontal position you'll feel the heavy g-force turning your legs to lead while getting dizzy from riding round and round the wall for 20 minutes. Even so, it'll be time for your tricks such as no hands, grabbing money proffered by spectators leaning into the arena or Australian Suicide –dangerously criss-crossing the paths of other riders.

Dangerous Idiot Odds	
Arrest	0
Injury	4
Death	1

Makes the BMX park look like a kindergarten

Open a Beer Bottle with Your Teeth

Let your laughing gear become operational.

Why else would God have given you such a strong set of pearly whites (or maybe yellows in your case), if not to put them to good use around the house. Learn these techniques and you'll never be searching for a bottle opener again (although you might have to dig out the Yellow Pages for a decent dentist).

Although your back molars are the strongest of your choppers and are great for chewing (see Eating a Lightbulb page 111), the front two incisors are the most useful for piercing and opening. To open a beer or similar bottle with a sharp-edged metal cap simply hook the cap, over the bottom incisors, close your mouth, bringing the top canines on to the top of the cap and take a firm grip. Now gently and repeatedly lift and lower the bottle, keeping it hooked on the tooth until you have worked the cap loose enough to remove it.

Useful – and you look cool at parties. Unless, of course, you end up with a bloody mess of a mouth, unattractive broken and chipped teeth and still no beer. Oh and the pressure could halt the flow of nutrients to the teeth, eventually leading to a particularly fetching grey smile. Still, that won't be for a while, there'll be a whole load of parties before then...

Dangerous Idiot Odds
Arrest 0
Injury 4
Death 0

Like they always said, you really are a tool...

The Moto Taxi Rally

A sofa on wheels – what could possibly go wrong?

It's the brand new adventure that's all the rage for dangerous idiots with too much time and too many intact bones – crossing extreme terrain on a vehicle barely capable of negotiating a new housing estate.

The Moto Taxi is a motor-powered rickshaw similar to the south-east Asian tuk-tuk. Invented in Peru and yet to be perfected anywhere, it is basically a weedy motorbike pulling a sofa on wheels – pretty incompatible with the backstreets of Lima and downright madness in the wilds of South America.

The Adventurists' annual Moto Taxi Junket goes from Peru to Paraguay via Brazil and Bolivia and takes in river crossings, mountains, jungle tracks and desert sand dunes. The moto-taxi reaches a maximum speed of about 20mph (32 kph), a lot less with three screaming idiots in the back and even less than that when faced with difficult terrain – which is basically all of the time.

The chances of injury are manifold – concussion, broken bones and lost limbs are distinct possibilities – and it's common to lose passengers from the death-trap sofa, see the vehicle plunge over a cliff top or have it break down in the wilderness (Haynes are yet to bring out a Moto Taxi manual).

Dangerous Idiot Odds
Arrest 2
Injury 4
Death 2

Sofa, so dangerous…

Part Three
It's a Dangerous World

Travel, they say, broadens the mind – it also provides
a fantastic playground for those who want to put their
mortal souls in danger. This selection of stunts, holiday
destinations and far-flung hellholes should be enough for
you to rip up your passport and stay home forever.

Illegally Entering the USA from Mexico

If you thought US passport control was tough, try the alternative – bandits, midnight river crossings, desert survival and vigilantes...

Dangerous Idiot Odds
Arrest 5
Injury 5
Death 2

Every year a million South Americans, desperate to reach a country where their only work will be as underpaid labourers and cleaners (and, just occasionally, hit R'n'B singers), risk life and limb to illegally enter the Land of the Free. Sounds just the adventure for Superidiot...

The border between the United States and Mexico runs along the Rio Grande in Texas and the desert in Arizona. Actually entering Uncle Sam's yard isn't really the problem – it's the crossing and finding your way to civilization that gets dangerous.

For a hefty $2000, "Coyotes" will take you across. Like coach party tourist guides with a side-business in kidnapping, assault, rape and murder, they'll show you where to wade across the Rio Grande, pack you in an overcrowded suffocating van or cut some of the razor wire at San Ysidro so you can crawl under the fence.

If you avoid the ruthless border bandits and manage to get across, your troubles really start. You'll find yourself in a desert wilderness in temperatures that can range from well above 104°F (40 °C) to below freezing at night: take a wrong turn and you could be walking for 50 miles (80 km) before you reach any sign of civilisation. You know when you're near though – you'll see the patrols of American vigilantes willing to give you a beating and send you straight back across the desert...

What d'you mean "it's alright, I'll get a visa"? Where's your spirit of adventure?

Survive the Worst Prison in the World

Only the toughest do time in the Bangkok Hilton – and come out sane.

You reckon you could cope with a stretch inside? Keep your head down, play a bit of pool and come out with a master's degree in nuclear physics? Not here you won't – welcome to Thailand's Bang Kwang, otherwise known the Bangkok Hilton.

Upon arrival at Bangkwang, prisoners are fitted with leg-irons that are welded to their legs for the first 6 to 18 months. So that's football on Saturday afternoon out. You'll then spend 14 hours a day locked up in a 20x13 ft (6x4 m) cell with 20 or so vicious, sick or mentally ill cellmates. There are no beds, you cannot avoid contact with the inmate sleeping next to you and the room is lit 24 hours a day by fluorescent bulbs.

You share the open toilet in the cell and wash with polluted water from the local river; the sewers are open too, and in monsoon season regularly flood the cell. Culinary standards won't trouble Michelin: once a day, the prison provides a meal of red rice with a thin watery soup with the odd fish head or tail.

Finally, with one in six of the 6,000 prisoners on death row awaiting death by injection or machine gun, often receiving only two hours notice of execution, it's unlikely you'll find any takers for a game of Monopoly.

Dangerous Idiot Odds
Arrest 0
Injury 2
Death 1

Unbearable conditions, barbaric torture and no soft toilet paper.
"I'll just stay the one night, thanks."

Send Yourself by Mail

Just hope they're careful where they stamp that postmark...

In the famous Flat Stanley books, when his parents baulk at the extortionate air fare, the half-inch thick boy is posted to his cousins in California. Now, admittedly, you won't slide quite so easily into an envelope and it might require quite an outlay in stamps – but hey, what a way to travel!

The Post Office and the US Mail have a maximum package weight of around 70lbs (32 kg), so unless you slim down a little you're going to have to contact a courier. Most are more obliging and will take you next-day delivery – just don't tell 'em it's you they're mailing.

Your first step is easy, the days of having to contort yourself and squat in a wooden box are over – these days you can get giant jiffy bags, the kind they use for refrigerators and pianos. They're strong and have plenty of padding to protect you when the posties start throwing you around. Make sure you address it first, get yourself some provisions, jump in and make yourself comfortable.

Anything to worry about while you are in transit? Well, first it's illegal; second, there's a chance you'll suffocate in the package; third you could face temperatures of –40°F (–40 °C) in the unpressurized hold of the plane and lastly, you know what they're like, they'll probably lose you! But it can be done. In 2003, New Yorker Charles McKinley, due to visit his father in Dallas, Texas, decided to "ship himself" rather than pay for a ticket. He managed to stay undetected right up to when he was dumped on his father's drive!

Dangerous Idiot Odds
Arrest 4
Injury 3
Death 2

With the price of air travel these days, no one will blame you…

Volcano Boarding

Brave the coughing mountain for the ride of your life.

Where do the snowboarders go once the snow has gone? Up the volcano. Bombing down a still active volcano has all the elements your adrenaline junkie requires – speed, thrills, skills, danger and, if you venture to the right spot, a chance of dying.

Nicaragua's Cerro Negro, the youngest volcano in Central America and one of the most active in the region, has become a magnet for orange jump-suited boarders seeking a bit of dangerous fun. First they must climb the 2,382ft (726 m) through sulphur fumes to the top of the still-smoking crater before sliding down the ash – settled from the last major eruption in 1999.

The ash is denser and stickier than snow and takes its toll on the calves and thighs, but nevertheless boarders can reach speeds of 50mph (80 kph). Spills are frequent and care has to be taken if you're to avoid your face being impaled on a rock.

Even more adventurous boarders have ventured to Tanna Island in South Vanuatu to brave Mount Yasur, one of the world's most active volcanos. Climbing past the memorials to deceased travellers who never made the top and being defened by the volcano's explosions, you realize the dangers not only of flying off your board at high speed, but also the very real risk of being struck by lava bombs the size of backpacks, overcome by toxic gas and caught in unpredictable avalanches emerging from the crater.

Dangerous Idiot Odds
Arrest 0
Injury 2
Death 1

Sure beats getting the skateboard out and scaring the shoppers at the precinct

The Pamplona Bull Run

Wild, angry bulls chasing thousands through a Spanish village – is this the maddest festival in the world?

On every daredevils list of things to do before they die, the Pamplona Bull Run has become a convention for mad idiots from across the world. Dressed in white with their natty red bandanas, these brave souls interrupt their drunken revelry for an hour or so to be chased through town by a herd of pent-up, aggressive, eager-for-Aussie-blood beasts.

Dating back to the 14th century and made famous by Ernest Hemingway in his novel *The Sun Also Rises*, the festival of San Fermin as it is formally known takes place every morning from 7–14 July. The rocket signalling the release of six fighting bulls and two herds of bullocks, is the cue for runners to scurry from the town square, down 2,710 ft (825 m) of cobbled streets in an attempt not to be this year's victims.

The average time of the run from start to finish is about three minutes, but with hundreds running it is impossible to make a mad dash. The most dangerous part of the course is Dead Man's Corner – a 90-degree turn where the bulls often lose their footing. These separated and confused bulls often go on the attack, charging or goring a hungover tourist who has stopped to get his breath.

The bull run is fenced off so the bulls can't escape, but runners can find gaps to squeeze through if they want to chicken out. It's worth considering – since 1924, over 200 have been seriously injured and 15 people have died.

Dangerous Idiot Odds	
Arrest	2
Injury	3
Death	1

If you think Red Bull is a good hangover cure, try a furious, charging, real-life bull...

Drive the Most Dangerous Road in the World

If ever there was a highway to hell...

The North Yungas Road. It sounds quite homely doesn't it? You could think of it running past the shops and the golf club onto quite a sharp mini-roundab... stop! This is a killer road – officially the most dangerous in the world.

Known as *El Camino de la Muerte*, (Road of Death) it runs 38 miles (61 km) from the highest capital in the world, La Paz, and plunges almost 11,810 ft (3,600 m) along narrow hairpin curves and 2,625 ft (800 m) sheer drops to Coroico. A fatal accident happens virtually every two weeks with 100-200 people coming a cropper there every year.

The road is little more than a single lane hacked out of the mountainside, bordered by 3,000 ft (915 m) cliffs. It is only 10.5 ft (3.2 m) wide, unpaved and muddy in many places and there's no guard rails to prevent you plunging over the edge. The area the road passes through is especially remote so when you do career down the mountain it can be days before anyone finds you.

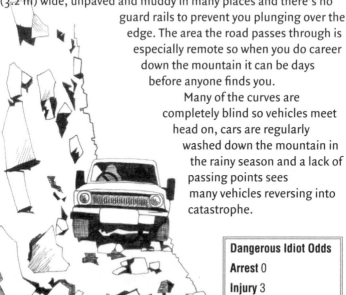

Many of the curves are completely blind so vehicles meet head on, cars are regularly washed down the mountain in the rainy season and a lack of passing points sees many vehicles reversing into catastrophe.

Dangerous Idiot Odds	
Arrest	0
Injury	3
Death	3

The North Yungas Road welcomes careful drivers – and kills uncareful ones

Camping on Snake Island

The island where you are never more than 3 ft (90 cm) from death...

Ah! The great outdoors – campfires, fresh air and nature all around. Take a trip to Ilha de Queimada Grande, an island off the coast of Brazil, and you will certainly find nature close-up. Here you really will be able to get away from it all – there are no inhabitants and no buildings, and the Brazilian Navy has expressly forbidden anyone from landing on the island.

An island paradise then? Well almost – if it wasn't for the estimated one to five snakes per 11 sq ft (1 sq m) on the island. And, these are not little grass snakes, these are golden lancehead snakes, a unique species of pit viper that is responsible for 90 percent of Brazilian snakebite-related fatalities – killing around 100 people a year. Over 1.5 ft (0.5 m) long, they possess a super-powerful fast-acting venom that melts the flesh around their bites.

In what sounds like the plot of a horror story, the island's last inhabitants – the family of the lighthouse keeper – are said to have fled in panic one night after snakes crawled in through their windows. Snared as they ran through the jungle by vipers dangling from tree branches, their bodies were supposedly found dotted around the island.

Dangerous Idiot Odds
Arrest 4
Injury 4
Death 4

Is that that the welcome hiss of the kettle on the campfire or…

A Holiday in Miyakejima

A perfect break for those who love the smell of farts...

Looking for the ideal holiday destination, somewhere out-of-the-way, exotic and interesting with a reasonable chance of coming home in a wooden box? Then look no further than the island of Miyakejima, part of the Izu Islands, a group of volcanic islands 112 miles (180 km) south of Tokyo.

There's plenty to do here – the island has incredible flora and fauna, great coral reefs, schools of dolphins and the inhabitants are famous for their *taiko* drum performances. And then there is Mount Oyama. You can't miss it, a sulphurous fuming monster volcano that is likely to spew forth at any time.

Mount Oyama has history. It killed 11 people in 1940, and erupted again in 1962 and 1983. Then, in August 2000, after the volcano had shot rocks 8,000 ft (2,440 m) in the air and covered the island in a cloud of smoke 5 miles (8 km) high, the entire population of around 3,000 people was evacuated from the island.

Four years later, residents were allowed to return but are now compelled to wear gas masks outside. The constant flow of sulphuric gas from the volcano not only makes the island smell like a million farts, but can cause serious respiratory problems. Alarms often sound at night as the levels of sulphur in the air dramatically increase. Best keep your bags packed – you could be leaving in a hurry.

Useful phrase: "Uchi ni kaeritai!" ("I want to go home!")

Swim the Yucatan Channel

Who can resist the challenge of the open sea?

There are some famous swimming feats around the world: the English Channel, crossed by hundreds of larded-up idiots every year; Turkey's Hellespont, the stretch of water separating Europe and Asia and first swam by Lord Byron in 1810 and the 75 ft (23 m) through screaming, peeing kids at the local lido. But few match the challenge of the Yucatan Channel that separates Cuba and Mexico.

For swimmers these waters are often treacherous, and sometimes fatal, due to the strong and unpredictable currents. Divers have been swept away and the sea predators – including tiger sharks and deadly jellyfish – are always present in the deep waters of the channel. And bear in mind that much of your swim will be in the dark – when the sharks are partial to a little snack.

It's not impossible. The swim of 122 miles (200 km) – equivalent to over six English Channels was achieved by long-distance swimming specialist Australian Susie Maroney in under 39 hours, so give yourself a couple of days to make it. However, she kind of cheated, swimming in a shark cage and in a special suit to protect her from jellyfish stings. I'd expect to see you set off with just your speedos and a packet of mints.

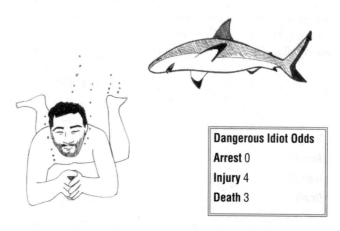

Dangerous Idiot Odds
Arrest 0
Injury 4
Death 3

Don't forget your water wings.

Become an Amazonian Warrior

Been bitten by the tribal bug? Are you sure?

Ants. They're pesky little beggars – getting in your sandwiches and crawling up your trouser legs. But, if you're going to become an Amazonian warrior you are going to have to get used to more than a few of these unpleasant creatures evil cousins – the bullet ants.

The bullet ant is the largest ant on Earth – around 1oin (25 cm) long and its sting is scientifically proven to be the most painful of any invertebrate, being 30 times more potent than that of a common wasp. The Satere-Mawe people of Brazil call it the "24-hour ant" because being pierced by its 0.5 in (5 mm) sting leads to 24 hours of intense pain.

This is why they use the bullet ant as part of the initiation rites to become a warrior. They sedate 400 of the creatures with a chloroform, stitching them into a mitten with their stingers pointing inwards. As the ants come round, the would-be warrior slips his hand into the glove and is required to keep it on for ten minutes.

The pain is said to be beyond belief – *Times* journalist Steve Backshall who underwent the ceremony wrote: "If there'd been a machete to hand, I'd have chopped off my arms to escape the pain." Initiates are said to suffer paralysis, comas and can shake uncontrollably for days – and they are expected to repeat the ordeal 20 times before they are true warriors.

Dangerous Idiot Odds
Arrest 0
Injury 5
Death 1

Oh well, the facepaint and the dancing looks fun...

Climb Mount Everest

"Because it's there" – the motto of the dangerous idiot.

Hardly a day goes by when there isn't news of yet another ascent of Everest. Surely it won't be long before there's an escalator and a café at the top. And yet they still tell us that high-altitude climbing is the most dangerous sport on earth?

But, before you pack your rucksack with some Kendall mint cake and a spare pair of socks, it might be worth glancing at the dangers. Although we're pretty sure there's no Yeti around, and the mountaineering isn't technically too difficult (there are even ladders for the tricky bits), there are some risks in climbing the 29,029 ft (8,848 m).

Around 180 of the 1300 climbers have died attempting to conquer the mountain. That's about one in six, so you'll be stepping over some corpses on the way up. Hypothermia, frostbite and pneumonia are all queuing up to get you; a wrong step and you're falling thousands of feet down a crevasse and even a broken leg can be fatal if the rescue helicopter can't find you.

Then there's Acute Mountain Sickness, a kind of hangover without any of the fun of the night before; High-altitude Cerebral Edema, an affliction that slows the brain (a bit like the "night before") and the Khumbu cough, so strong it can tear chest muscles or break ribs – and guarantees at least a week off work.

And even when you get to the top, you can't see much. Take your glasses off and the ultra-violet exposure will do serious damage to your eyes.

Dangerous Idiot Odds
Arrest 0
Injury 5
Death 3

That's what you call a mountain with altitude...

Survive a Plane Crash

From the burning wreckage crawls one, slightly dishevelled but intact idiot...

If this is your ambition it could be a difficult one to achieve. Plane crashes are extremely rare; so your best bet is to head to Russia, China or Turkey where the stats indicate that you are more likely to take the plunge.

Over 90 percent of plane crashes have survivors, you just have to make sure one of them is you. First, carefully consider where you are going to sit, maybe choose the rear (you never see a plane reversing into anything!) as many experts suggest you have a 40 percent better chance of survival there. Others suggest you sit by the wing – a reinforced part of the plane, near to the exit doors.

Before you take your seat, examine how the doors open and count the number of rows to the exit. If smoke fills the plane you won't be able to see and will have to find your way out by memory. Next, watch carefully how you fasten your seatbelt. Many crashees forget how to release it and waste time looking for a button in the crucial minutes after a crash.

Now prepare your crash brace position, cross your hands on the seat in front of you, put your head against your hands and get down as low as possible limiting the "jackknife" effect on impact. Ready for the crash? The golden period for escape lasts only up to about two minutes, so stay on your feet and head for the exit – over the seats if necessary. If there's smoke around, crouch low, put a damp cloth over your mouth and nose (the crutch of your by now wet trousers will do) and get the hell out of there quickly.

And don't stand around chatting, run for cover – you can worry about who's going to eat whom later...

Remember, it's not who gets out alive first – it's who gets the first post on Twitter

Part Four
Only For Idiots

There's always one, isn't there? In every crowd some fearless idiot steps forward ready to humiliate or injure himself for the public good. Something in his genes makes him take it too far – like eating stuff off the sidewalk, climbing so far up a tree that he can't get down or any of the following damn-fool ideas...

Alien Abduction

Who's up for a little extra-terrestrial torture?

Are you a complete loner? Do you sometimes hear voices in your head? Do you obsessively watch tedious sci-fi fantasy movies? Have you a pudding-bowl haircut and an ill-fitting anorak? If so, you probably think you've been abducted by aliens already, but for the rest of us it is but an aspiration.

It appears that alien abduction has its drawbacks – you are whisked away without warning (there could be something good on TV), brainwashed, subjected to complex physical and psychological procedures and sometimes mistakenly returned to the wrong place – but it's not all bad, abductees claim they get to chat to their inter-galactic kidnappers, be given a tour around the UFO and have all memory of the pain removed.

It seems impossible to volunteer for abduction but they seem to happen most often just before dropping off to sleep or in the middle of late-night car journeys. If you catch a glimpse of bright lights and humanoid-type figures, then the chances are you are off on a trip of a lifetime.

Compared to many of the escapades in this book the chances of serious injury are slight, but who knows what goes on up there? We're dangerous idiots and not afraid of a little genital probing though it's not like you get to remember any of it, just the odd flashback and a general sense of paranoia and estrangement from the human race.

Dangerous Idiot Odds

Arrest 0 (but very possible certification)

Injury 3

Death 0

None of your mates will believe you – but that's nothing new is it?

Pulling Your Own Teeth

An activity that is not only dangerous but can save you a sizeable sum at the dentist.

Toothache can be unbearable, and so can dental fees – but there is a solution. DIY dentistry is an incredibly painful, potentially damaging and damn fool option. Just say, "aaaaaahhh" and we'll begin...

Back in the days when there were no waiting rooms full of last year's *Grazia* magazines, black leather chairs, hairy-nostrilled Australians staring down at you or strange pink liquid to swash and spit, if you needed a tooth out, you took as much alcohol as you could muster and got to work with a pair of rusty pliers.

What? Flinching at the idea of wrenching away at the rotting molar for a couple of hours? Then go for the old short, sharp shock option – tie a piece of string to the tooth, tie the other end to an open door and kick the door shut.

That might work for a toddler's loose milk tooth but it's unlikely to shift any of your hampsteads. You'll need to tie it to something really heavy – like a car battery – which you then chuck out the window of a five-storey building or hitch it to a revved-up Harley Davidson that tears off up the road. You should lose the tooth alright, but chances are you'll lose part of jaw as well.

Alternatively, you could just see if you could get a punch in the mouth.

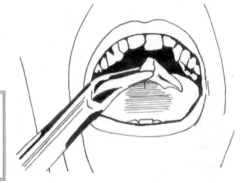

```
Dangerous Idiot Odds
Arrest 0
Injury 5
Death 1
```

Blood, pain and a whole lot of remedial dentistry work – but you'll cure that toothache

Shark Attack

Open those cage doors and take a dip with the ultimate ocean predator...

Every year thousands of tourists show just how brave they are by climbing into a cage and being lowered into shark-infested waters. But, with only 60 or so shark attacks recorded each year – of which only around five are fatal – surely anyone wanting a real adrenaline rush would risk a face to face encounter with the terror of the deep?

We need to bring the odds down a little, so you've got more chance of meeting a fishy end than winning the lottery. Head for Florida, statistically the place you're most likely to be attacked and enter the sea at dusk when sharks are at their most active. Try taking a board with you (they have a penchant for surfers) and do a little splashing to attract attention.

Now, make sure there is blood: cut your finger or shove a nice bloody steak down your pants – sharks can smell the tiniest amount of blood from over 1 mile (1.6 km) away and easily follow it back to its source.

Sharks generally like "ambush attacks", taking out their prey in one strike, so watch out for your legs disappearing in an instant. If you come face to face with the beast try hitting it on the nose – this might make it go away or could really piss it off. If it bites, don't play dead. Forget the Queensbury rules, go for the eyes and gills and claw and bite for your life.

Dangerous Idiot Odds
Arrest 0
Death 1
Injury 3

When you hear the dum...dum...dum music, start to panic

Buried Alive

It's a common enough nightmare but what sort of idiot would voluntarily be interred beneath?

It was a stunt that even the great Harry Houdini vowed never to attempt again after being buried alive in Santa Ana, California, in 1917. Buried 6 ft (1.8 m) under in a dark, airless and claustrophobic coffin, knowing the only way out is by somehow fighting through a ton of soil? It's a stunt only the truly brave or stupefying stupid would try...

With the earth packed around, restricting the air supply, the oxygen in your coffin will run out after about two hours max. In this time you would need to expend a fair amount of energy kicking and pushing the coffin lid open. If you succeed you then face the unbearable pressure of the soil and an exhausting frantic scramble as you desperately attempt to push the soil around you and force your body upwards.

What if you were instead trapped under a crumbling building? How long could you hope to last then? In the 2010 Haiti earthquake, emergency operations were called off 11 days after the ground shook. This is about as long as a fit and well-nourished person would live.

Dangerous Idiot Odds
Arrest 1
Injury 2
Death 4

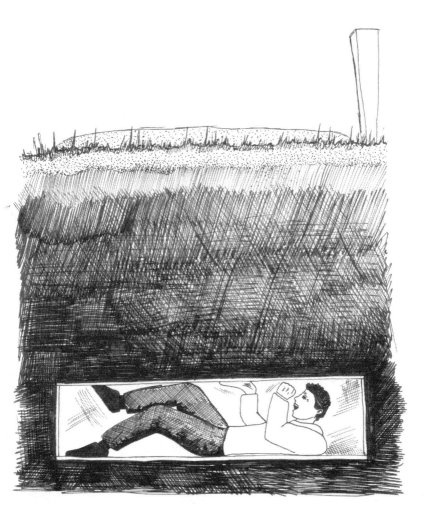

Hello? Hello? – Anyone coming to dig me out? Hello?

Biting the Head off a Live Snake

Try saying that with a mouthful of reptile

Chickens have had it rough for too long – circus sideshow acts, bored squaddies, Hell's Angels and rock stars have all had their turn at chewing through the poor foul's neck and watching the headless body frantically run around. But let's even the fight a little – and pick on a creature whose might just bite back...

You'll not be the first to sink your teeth into the legless reptile – in America, stories are rife of rednecks taking revenge on rattlesnakes by biting them back or of fairground geeks (originally a name for carnival performers who undertake repulsive acts) performing the act for money. But you'll almost certainly be able to boast of being the first on your block.

Your chances of injury will depend on which species of the critters you pick on: a little grass snake won't hurt but hardly puts you in the daredevil field, whereas something poisonous like an adder or a rattler could land you with a trip to hospital. You'll find a snake's skin a lot more difficult to get your teeth through than any chicken neck, and that means more time for it to turn the tables on you.

Anything else you need to know? Only that a snake's head can go on living for an hour after it has been severed – it's reflex bite still well capable of sinking it's fangs in you.

Dangerous Idiot Odds
Arrest 3
Injury 4
Death 1

It's cruel, illegal and damn foolish – but that's never stopped a true idiot

Auto-Bungee Jump

Mirror, signal, manoeuvre – ahhhhhh!

Looking for a few more thrills than doing 35mph (55 kph) between speed cameras in your Astra? How about taking your four-wheeled friend for the drive of its life – on a 330 ft (100 m) bungee jump! It will of course require a little preparation – wielding attachments for the elastic to the back of the car, fixing it to a large crane and checking your insurance will cover you, but just imagine plunging through the air in a two-ton lump of metal knowing it will suddenly stop, go into a rapid climb then start to fall again...

According to the laws of gravity you should be able to go from 0-130mph (210 kph) in about six seconds, however you will need to factor in wind resistance, meaning you'll reach a terminal velocity of around 90mph (150 kph). There will be no option of putting the brakes on to slow things down so you'd best check your seatbelt and maybe wear a crash helmet just in case. Put the car into gear and slowly drive it off the platform into mid-air... praying that the garage has done a decent job with the welding and that the bungees can take the weight.

Dangerous Idiot Odds
Arrest 2
Injury 4
Death 3

No traffic cops, no speed cameras –
just a 33 ft (100 m) fall and a severe case of whiplash

Jump Through a Glass Window

Are you ready for a great leap forward?

The flames are getting closer – there's no other way out but to throw yourself through the window. You cross your arms in front of your face and launch yourself through the plate glass. With just a few small scratches you dust yourself down, look back at your silhouette cut out of the glass and run on...

In your dreams... Chances are that, if you could build up the speed and force to break through the glass, you'd emerge with large pieces of the window protruding from parts of your body and various gashes that will take the number of stitches into the hundreds. As you break through the glass, the sharp broken edges would lacerate your skin and equally jagged, unsupported pieces would cut with a velocity that could sever an artery or a limb.

But what if it was safety glass? This is thermally toughened glass, which is less likely to cause harm as it breaks into small fragments rather than shards. It is possible to break, but being five times as tough as plate glass and especially designed to withstand impact you've more chance of ending up with a broken arm, a bloody nose and still be in the room.

But that's science and what do they know? In 2007 a burglar in Tyneside, England, broke into a school by using his head to ram the glass door and diving through. He escaped with a plasma TV and barely a scratch.

Dangerous Idiot Odds
Arrest 4
Injury 4
Death 2

That's why they invented the door!

Supermarket Joust

Back to the age of chivalry and senseless skirmish...

It was the appointed time. He looked through the swirling mists and caught the steely look of his adversary's eye. He gripped his weapon, flexed his knees and took a firm grasp on his trusty steed. "Brave Sir Idiot," up went the cry. "Win the tournament."

When a knight won his spurs in the stories of old, he suffered no 24-hour security guards, ASBO laws or health and safety regulations, but let's not let them put us off our modern-day feats of valour and immense stupidity.

Supermarket joust takes place in an empty car park – early morning or a Sunday afternoon when the shop has closed and there are no cars apart from an incompetent learner practising his three-point turns. You'll need to borrow a couple of supermarket trolleys – not one with a wonky wheel – have a couple of mops as lances, and you and your combatant will need "squires" to push you and call the ambulance when necessary.

Perch in your trolley – either kneeling in the trolley or sitting on the edge – with your mop at the ready. At the "herald" (have you got a mate with a bugle?), your squire pushes you as fast as possible towards the oncoming opponent. As you pass, try to knock each other out of the trolley. If both parties remain seated, you must turn around and charge again.

Dangerous Idiot Odds
Arrest 3
Injury 4
Death 0

Who will win the sweet lady's favour – or at least a couple of pints in the boozer?

Crossing the English Channel by Pedalo

Forget roll-on off, roll-off, this day trip is self-propelled...

It's only a 21 mile (34 km) divide, but it has foiled the Spanish Armada, German U-boats and a Frenchman in an inflatable. But you are made of sterner stuff and are seated in a plastic beach pedalo, pedalling for all your worth.

You will need, of course, a hilariously shaped pedalo (a whale could put the wind up other shipping), a bucket for bailing out the gallons of water you'll take on board and a fair amount of stamina. At an average speed of 2 mph (3 kph), you – and a mate – are going to be pedalling for at least 10 hours – double or quadruple that if the wind and tides are against you.

You will also need to bear in mind that the Dover Strait is the busiest shipping lane in the world – and much of the traffic is made up of difficult-to-manoeuvre, massive high-speed ferries that take several miles to stop or turn. Then there are the strong tides, sandbanks, shoals, steep breaking waves and rapidly changing weather conditions. Steering and navigation might also prove a small obstacle but carefully plan your route and, if in doubt, just follow one of the 13-year-old girls constantly swimming across the divide.

Since it is illegal to take a pedalo further than 985 ft (300 m) out to sea, you could have the coastguard on your tail as well – still, with a little bit of frantic pedalling I'm sure you could outrun them...

Dangerous Idiot Odds
Arrest 5
Injury 2
Death 2

Come in number 12 your time is up.. number 12?...number 12!!!

Let's Go Storm Chasing

Come on! It's only weather...

Since *Twister* roared onto the movie screens in 1995, storm chasing has become an American national sport with hundreds of hunters leaping into their cars as soon as a weather forecaster even utters the word "torna.."

The tornado is the holy grail of storm hunters, and the appearance of a "twister" heralds almighty chases across Tornado Alley – the American mid-west states. The F5 tornado – the most intense damage category on the Fujita and Enhanced Fujita damage scales – occurs only once a twice a year, but these are the cup finals; an orgy of weather-driven destruction with a distinct possibility of personal injury or death.

As dangerous as it is speeding down roads attempting to catch a tornado that moves around 40mph (65kph) – the real thrill is in "punching the core". This is when you drive right through the curtains of rain into the heart of the "nader" (chaser shorthand for tornado). Here you'll find lightening, driving rain and "gorilla hail" – hailstones the size of baseballs coming at you at over 100mph.

Then there are the winds. Tornados can have winds exceeding 200 or even 300 mph (320 or 480 kph) and have tossed a man over 1,000 ft (305 m).

Get out of the car and you'll be dodging flying debris and household objects, stay in and you could be thrown as far as 330 ft (100 m). But get some footage of it and you'll definitely make the local news.

Dangerous Idiot Odds
Arrest 5
Injury 4
Death 3

Admit it – who hasn't wanted to shout "It's a twister! It's a twister!"

Get Caught in an Avalanche

Spice up your skiing holiday with a life or death scenario...

Down the hill, back up the ski-lift, down the hill again, back...
still seven hours until you get your boots off and a glass of
gluwein down you. Skiing can be so boring sometimes, and you
yearn for the thrill of movie-style avalanche to speed your way
back to the chalet.

Avalanches can be a terrifying ordeal and claim over
150 lives each year worldwide with hundreds more injured or
trapped. They occur in slopes of between 30 and 40 degrees –
the intermediate ski slopes (blue square runs of America or red
pistes in Europe) – especially when there are large amounts (over
10 in / 25 cm) of new snow, a heavy thaw or overnight high winds.
The tell-tale signs are cracks in the snow, creaking noises and
someone shouting "Avalanche!"

The average avalanche travels at a speed of around 80
mph (128 kph) so there isn't much chance of escape. Once you
are overtaken by the snow you should try to swim with the flow
to the edge or at least try to get some part of your body above
the surface. Now it's a battle for your life against suffocation or
hypothermia. The sooner you are found the better – the chances
of survival are estimated at 85 percent if you are found within 15
minutes, 50 percent within 30 minutes and 20 percent within one
hour.

Dangerous Idiot Odds
Arrest 0
Injury 2
Death 4

At least it'll shut that flippin' yodeller up

Jackhammer Pogo

If you like a pogo stick, you'll love this.

The Jackhammer, also known as a pheumatic drill, is a building tool driven by compressed air and used to break up rock, pavement and concrete. It's a dangerous machine, emitting ear-piercing sound (over 100 decibels) and driving downwards with a massive force of 100 lbs (45 kg). Surely this is too good an opportunity to miss? Because, basically, this is a supercharged pogo stick pounding up and down 25 times each second, hitting the ground around 1,500 times every minute. Master the art of riding the thing and you'll be the King of the Idiots.

You'll have to make a few adaptations to the drill. Tape a rest for your knees halfway up the drill and fix something on the end of the drill to stop it digging – a special plate used for flattening ground would be ideal. Put on your ear defenders and some thick trousers to stop your legs getting burnt, then start the jackhammer, climb on and cling on for dear life.

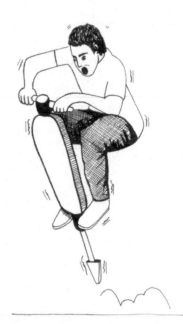

If the impact doesn't smash your knees and the vibration doesn't leave you without control of your hands, you might just have invented the greatest craze of the 21st century.

Dangerous Idiot Odds
Arrest 2
Injury 4
Death 1

Coming soon…. Jackhammer stunt riding

Part Five
The Sporting Chancer

Across the ages the sporting arena has seen great feats of skill, endurance and bravery. But it's also the ideal venue for an utter idiot. Elsewhere, folk look with disdain and disrespect at the dangerously stupid but the sporting life offers glory, adulation and many a trip to intensive care...

80

BASE Jumping

The answer to man's greatest quest? Or just some idiot chucking himself off a big building?

People can develop anything into a sport – like jumping off tall buildings. All you need is a parachute and no fear of heights and you can become a world-class BASE jumper. Just throw yourself off one of each of these locations – a building, antennae, span (i.e. a bridge) and earth (a cliff) – and you get a special number to prove how daring you are.

And it is pretty daring. Jump from 500 feet (152 m) and it takes about 12 seconds to ride to the ground with an open chute – 6 seconds if your chute doesn't open. Enough time to think about your future as a vegetable but no time to open any reserve chute. And then there's the surprise gust of wind that can hurl you back against the building. All in all they reckon there's around one fatality per 60 participants!

The fun is finding the best place to jump from. Most owners of tall buildings are not too keen on idiots flinging themselves off their roof, so you need to be sneaky. But out in the wilds there are mountains, cliffs, caves – all beautiful places to end your days.

Dangerous Idiot Odds
Arrest 3
Injury 3
Death 3

Why did they build tall buildings if they didn't want us to jump off them?

Human Trebuchet

What do you call a bungee that doesn't come back? Step up for the human catapult...

In medieval times they came up with the idea of a massive catapult known as a trebuchet. Consisting of an arm, a sling and a counterweight, the device was used to throw missiles and even dead, diseased bodies over the walls of a fortress.

Thus inspired, the Dangerous Sports Club – inventors of the bungee jump – built their own human trebuchet aiming to launch live people to about 82 ft (25 m) into the air at around 45 mph (70 kph), propelling them into a safety net around 98 ft (30 m) away.

Armed with a neck brace and a crash helmet, all you need do is strap on the harness, get fixed up to the sling and say your prayers. Pretty soon you'll be flying through the air like a screaming, overgrown squirrel, crashing into the net and back in the sling before you can say "spinal chord contusion."

The catch? Ah. Well, how's your physics and algebra? The Dangerous Sports Club is full of boffins from Oxford and Cambridge who carefully worked out the speed, trajectory and force of the flight when positioning the net. And even they sometimes got it wrong – notoriously in the death of a young man in 2002 (which led to the sport being made illegal). So what chance do you give you and your mates with one maths GCSE between you?

Dangerous Idiot Odds
Arrest 3
Injury 3
Death 2

Four seconds of ecstatic flight, a lifetime of back trouble...

Bushkazi

Looking for a game that will really get your goat?

The national sport of Afghanistan is bushkazi, a sport as anarchic, wild and brutal as the country itself often appears. The object of the game is simple – to pick up the carcass of a beheaded, cut off at the knees and disembowelled goat or calf and ride away from the other players. Sounds easy enough, but there are hundreds of other players armed with whips and sticks – and not just for use on the horses.

The good news is that unlike rugby there aren't millions of intricate rules to learn. In fact there aren't any rules. Whipping the face isn't considered good form, but kicking, whipping hands and knocking riders off their horses is all part of the fun. It is, as they say, a man's game – especially as women are banned from playing or watching.

As a newcomer you probably won't see the carcass for the dust being kicked up but get anywhere near it and you risk bruising, broken bones and being severely trampled when you are pulled off your horse. When the game's over, get on with the handshakes and "well played mate" and get the hell out. Stick around for the "afters" and you'll often find the game has escalated into a real tribal or ethnic battle where the sticks are replaced with guns and no-one's smiling anymore...

Dangerous Idiot Odds
Arrest 0
Injury 5
Death 2

A cross between polo and an after-hours fight outside the kebab shop...

Rough Stock Riding

A job that lasts as long as it took you to read this sentence, is full of mythical machismo and can make you a millionaire! Where do you sign on?

They call it "the most dangerous eight seconds in sport". Riding bareback, not on wild animals but on horses and bulls bred specifically to be as vicious and brutal as possible. Eight seconds to hang on with just one hand to a thin rope attached to a 2,000 lb (900 kg) beast that is writhing and bucking with hate and frustration.

The "rough stock" events – which include bronc and bull riding – are one of the biggest draws of professional rodeo tournaments and the successful riders are big stars. Succeed and you've got it made: fail and you face, at best, a humiliating retreat from the arena still in your chaps.

In the pen you'll settle on the bull's back, wrap your rope around the bull's girth, loop the end around your hand and nod. As the gate opens, the bull lunges out of the chute, spinning, jumping, kicking, lunging and rearing. All you have to do to impress the judges is stay in control.

Basically, it's not whether you get hurt, but when and how bad: bull riders suffer one "significant injury" for every 15 events – concussion, punctured lungs or a mess of broken bones. Still, a man's gotta do...

Dangerous Idiot Odds	
Arrest	0
Injury	5
Death	2

Try this challenge and you're a top dangerous idiot – no bull

Fighting a Duel

Get on that flight to Paraguay – best get a one-way ticket, just in case...

French writers (Proust) do it, American presidents (Lincoln, Jackson) do it, great cowboys do it (the Good, the Bad and the Ugly), let's do it – let's fight a duel.

A duel starts with an offended party offering a challenge – "apologize or fight" – and ends on the "field of honour" with one of the duelists dead or unable to fight on. For years, it was a means for the upper classes to settle their differences, but over the last 150 years has gradually been banned in every civilized country in the world – except Paraguay where duelling is still legal - providing you are a registered blood donor!

There is, however, an accepted way in which the duels are fought, based on rules agreed in Ireland in 1777 and generally adopted around the world. This codo duello establishes that:

- The challenged can apologize for the slight or choose weapons.
- The challenger chooses the location.
- If swords are used, the fight continues until "one is well blooded, disabled or disarmed".
- If pistols are selected, the challenger decides the number of paces between them – usually from 10 to 30.
- If no one is hurt on the first shot, the seconds agree whether an additional shot should be taken. Unlike Europeans, Americans prefer dueling to the death.
- The doctor's fee is paid by the challenger.

Dangerous Idiot Odds
Arrest 4
Injury 4
Death 3

A chivalrous, civilized means of settling an argument, it sure beats an unsavoury scrap by the bins in the pub car park…

Running on Ice

Cold, slippery and an accident waiting to happen...

Anyone who has ever lost his footing on a frosty patch on the way to the shops will realize how difficult it is to sprint across sheet ice, and yet the world record for running 328 ft (100 m) on ice is an amazing 17.35 seconds. Time to avoid the skate hire queue, sneak onto your local ice rink and start practising – how difficult can it be?

The key to successful ice-running is to maintain your balance by remaining upright and measured with no sudden changes of direction or speed. The ideal ice running posture is identical to that of a normal sprinter but even more emphasized – your back should be straight with your arms hovering by your side.

You know those flat-footed people who look like penguins when they run? Try to do that – you'll look pretty stupid but balance that out with sitting in A & E with a wet arse and a broken arm. Take short strides and land on as much as your foot as possible. Don't push off with the balls of the feet or your toes, lift each foot well clear of the ground at each step, bringing your knees up to 90 degrees to your body. Now, just maybe, you can avoid that undignified sprawl across the ice.

Dangerous Idiot Odds
Arrest 0
Injury 3
Death 1

Are you sure the only skid marks are on the ice?

Shin Kicking

The ancient and noble art of taking a lump out of someone's leg.

A fine old English tradition, the game of shin kicking is known to have taken place since the 18th century and is said to have drawn crowds of 30,000. Back in the 15th century, a number of British villages had their own shin-kicking champions, and contenders would toughen up their shins by taking hammers to them.

To play the game, competitors take their opponents firmly by the shoulders and attempt to take a chunk out of their shins. If they succeed in getting a kick in – as judged by a referee, known as a Stickler – they are rewarded with an attempt to throw their adversary to the ground and so win the tie.

The modern version of this game as practised annually at the Cotswold Olympick Games, is but a lily-livered, softy boys' option where they permit competitors to protect their shins with straw and even encourage them to shove as much down their trouser legs as possible.

The Dangerous Idiot, of course, would shun such niceties and return to the refined, sadomasochistic code of the game, where unprotected shin kickers wore hobnailed boots with metal toecaps or even have nails protruding from the sides. OK, some kickers ended up crippled for life but it was a man's game in those days...

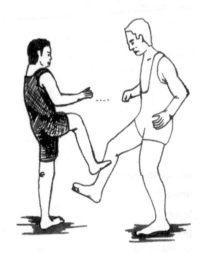

Dangerous Idiot Odds
Arrest 1
Injury 3
Death 0

Go on, have a go... you'll get a kick out of this

Competitive Apnea

The dangerous idiot's version of holding your breath for as long as possible.

Remember the first time you jumped off the high board at the swimming pool? It wasn't the jump that was really scary but the underwater panic that you might not have enough breath to get back to the surface. Multiply that fear by a thousand and you have Competitive Apnea...

It's really just holding your breath until you are about to faint made into a sport – except instead of feeling a little dizzy, you find yourself deep under water and with no option but to drown.

Competitors head out to sea and, holding onto a weighted sled, descend to a depth from which they think they can make the surface. Letting go of the weight they swim like hell for a breath of air. World records see the divers descending to over 656 ft (200 m) before ascending, holding their breath for five or six minutes.

With a handful of high-profile deaths among participants in recent years, Competitive Apnea is no sport for the faint-hearted. You risk drowning obviously, but also death by Shallow Water Blackout, when there is an insufficient amount of carbon dioxide to activate the body's natural impulse to breathe – not to mention sinus squeeze, eardrum explosion and hypervention blackout.

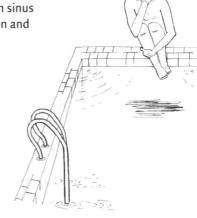

Dangerous Idiot Odds
Arrest 0
Injury 3
Death 4

If I were you I'd stick to looking for your soap in the bath

Street Luge

The most dangerous fun you can have lying down?

When it comes to devising terrifying, dangerous sports the human (or, in this case, *boredus teenagerum*) imagination knows no bounds. How else could you explain a pursuit where someone lays on a piece of tin on wheels and propels themselves down a hill without brakes?

That's street luge, a one- or two- person sled: lying on your back on a modified 8 ft (2.4 m) skateboard, taking on the steepest hill you can find. Keep your toes pointed, head down and body as flat and level as possible, you can reach speeds of 40–98 mph (64–157 kph). To brake, you simply stick a foot out and watch a hundred quid's worth of trainer go up in smoke.

A street luge is steered by leaning to one side. As they are lying only a few centimeters from the tarmac this often leads to shoulders and elbows making contact with the road surface. Shredded skin, ground-down bones and dislocated shoulders are commonplace in the sport.

Doing over 30 mph (48 kph) on major hills is usually a speeding offence, but with little control you've got a great chance of spilling, hitting a wall or coming face to face with a vehicle a lot bigger than yourself. Head injuries and deaths are as much as part of the game as twisted ankles are for tennis players.

Dangerous Idiot Odds
Arrest 3
Injury 4
Death 3

Keeping the transplant service going – they don't call street lugers "donors" for nothing!

Inuit Ear Pulling

Could this be the most excruciatingly painful sport ever?

What's your pain threshold like? If you cry like a baby when you get a paper cut you'd best sit this one out, but if your ears were toughened up by being twisted by sadistic schoolteachers, this might be your chance to go for gold.

The Ear Pull is a traditional Inuit endurance sport and sometime event at the Northern Games, held each summer in the Northwest Territorries. Recent years have found the game banned from many Arctic competitions because of the excruciating pain and the squeamishness of spectators. In the last tournament in which it was permitted, three of the ear-pull competitors were sent to hospital for stitches.

In the Ear Pull, two competitors sit opposite other, their legs straddled and intertwined. A 2 ft (60 cm) long length of string, similar to thick, waxed dental floss, is looped behind their ears, connecting the right ear to right ear, or left to left. At the signal, the competitors slowly lean backward, pulling the loop of string tighter and tighter behind their ears.

The pain is incredible and increasingly unbearable as the string cuts in deeper – the ears turning bright red and then purple, then stretching and crumpling. Only when the string slides off, or one of the competitors can't take the agony anymore, is the game over.

Dangerous Idiot Odds

Arrest 0

Injury 4

Death 0

But you've got to be Inuit to win it!

Become a Cheerleader

Have you got what it takes – gleaming teeth, supple limbs and neck brace?

Forget rugby, Aussie rules, boxing and no-holds barred tiddlywinks, the most dangerous sport in the world is cheerleading. Yep, the shiny teeth and bared legs of the all-American girl-next-door are in deadly peril. So get yourself into your spandex vest top and mini skirt, grab those pompoms and get cheering...

The tumbles, dances, jumps, cheers, and stunts inevitably take their toll on knees, shoulders and ankles but it's the head, neck and back injuries that make the football sidelines a dangerous place. Around 28,000 serious injuries — those involving death or disability caused by head or spine trauma – occur every year in US cheerleading.

The biggest threat of injury occurs in the cheerleader's stunts – the human pyramids, basket tosses and other gymnastic routines. Many squads perform 30-40 of these in a 3-5 minute display. These stunts require members of the squads to throw a teammate – the flyer – about 15 ft (5 m) in the air, and once the flyer has struck a pose, catch her again.

It's an impressive adrenaline-pumping routine but remember that the flyer is relying on a bunch of teenagers with their minds more on spots, boyfriends and chocolate than catching a 7 stone (45 kg) human missile. Hence the broken bones, paralysis and death. Be warned!

Dangerous Idiot Odds
Arrest 0
Injury 3
Death 1

You're right – stick to darts, it's so much safer

Naked Paintball

We're going on a bare hunt...

Paintball? It's very nearly like real war isn't it? You get a gun, get to roll around in long grass and shoot unsuspecting bozos on the backside and laugh as they leap around. OK, it's not really like war at all.

Anyone who has played the "sport" will know that getting shot hurts a little. The little paint shot can fire out of that rifle at around 300 ft (90 m) per second – it's like having a wet tennis ball thrown at you really hard. Sometimes you get left with a bruise or a welt but basically the pain goes away after a minute or so.

All naked paintball does is up the ante a little – making it that bit more exciting and a damn site more painful. Crawling around the undergrowth in your birthday suit might feel pretty uncomfortable but it's not as bad as the alternative – getting shot in the scrubland!

The eyes and face will present the real hazard – get shot in the mush and you could be facing blindness. Those with a little yellow in their bellies might want a change in the rules to allow participants to wear a mask or goggles – but beware, you could end up looking ridiculous!

Dangerous Idiot Odds
Arrest 4
Injury 4
Death 0

Putting the 'pain' into paintball

Invent a Martial Art

The wise one he say "go on, give him a kick up the jacksi!"

There's an old joke that centres around a chap saying he is a black belt in Feng Shui. But what if you could invent your own martial art and become a deadly proponent? You'll need a snappy name that sounds like it came from the Far East, a pompous moral code and, most importantly, some b**stard moves that could really hurt someone.

For the latter you could pick from some of the most deadly combat styles around the world. Take some from Krav Maga – the hand-to-hand combat technique practised by the Israeli Defence Force includes creating distractions and quickly follows up with bare-knuckle fighting, eye-gouging, gonad-kicking, ear-pulling and anything that will cause pain quickly and intensely. Throw in some Dim Mak death touches – blows to pressure points that incapacitate or kill an opponent (similar to that practised by *Star Trek*'s Mr. Spock) and add some of the crippling joint-locks and choke-holds of Brazilian Ju-Jitsu and you are nearly there.

You'll need a fair bit of meditation, bowing, salt throwing and pretending to be very respectful to your opponents while waiting to deal them an agonizing blow to the groin – and never admit you're looking for someone to practice your moves on, insist it's all purely self-defence!

Dangerous Idiot Odds
Arrest 4
Injury 4
Death 1

"What? There's only six of you? Bring it on…"

Off-Piste Zorbing

Just you and your hamster ball rolling free.

Extreme sports are all well and good, but once the health and safety brigade get to visit half the fun is taken out. Take zorbing – a potentially fantastic experience of rolling downhill in a giant transparent hamster ball, made tame by the harnesses, gentle slopes and controlled runs of corporate team building events.

On a commercial zorbing slope, the best you can achieve is around 15mph (24 kph) on an 820 ft (250 m) run. OK for the office day out but no big deal for your average idiot. So take your ball to a ski resort in the summer – it'll be a task getting it on the ski lift but the ride down will be sensational.

The world records for zorbing are set at 1,870 ft (570 m) for the longest run and 32.3mph (52 kph) for the fastest recorded speed, but manage to get moving down, say, Mont Blanc's Vallee Blanche or The Wall in Alvoriaz and you'll knock these to a cocked hat. Of course, negotiating several miles at speeds of over 60mph (95 kph) won't be easy. Concussion, bruising and dizziness could all impair your ability to steer and crashing at speed will test the strength of your ball.

Mad? Reckess? Impossible? Maybe. But it's idiots throughout history who have pushed the boundaries. In ten years time it'll be a management training exercise.

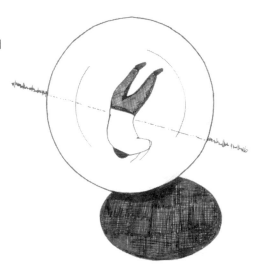

```
Dangerous Idiot Odds
Arrest 4
Injury 5
Death 2
```

Have you got the ball for this one?

Escalator Skiing

The men's indoor downhill – at a station near you...

It's the best fun you can have with two planks of wood – but going skiing can be such a tiresome business – the expensive resorts, the packed ski runs, the permanently tanned, good-looking instructors chatting up your girlfriend... But if this idea catches on, all you need is a trip to your local shopping mall with your skis (and maybe a helmet).

In 2007, a Norwegian daredevil skied down an escalator in London's Angel tube station with a camera strapped to his head and posted the video of his stunt on the net. He took just ten seconds to cover the 195 ft (60 m) escalator and though London Underground denounced him "dangerous and irresponsible", nobody was injured.

Anyone looking for a longer ride could take a trip to the Wheaton station of the Washington Metro subway system where the longest escalator in the western hemisphere is 508 ft (155 m) long or even the Park Pobedy station on the Moscow Metro 410 ft (125 m). Build up enough speed to negotiate the links between the escalators at Hong Kong's Central to Mid-Level system and you could enjoy a great half mile (0.8 km) ride from top to bottom.

There's one more great advantage of escalator skiing – there's no long queue for a chair lift, just cross over, ride back up to the top and start again...

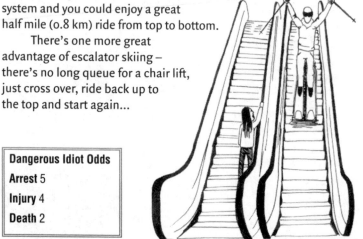

Dangerous Idiot Odds
Arrest 5
Injury 4
Death 2

It could be an Olympic sport by 2020 so get practicing

Part Six
Are You Out of Your Mind?

There are many forces that can drive a man to extreme behaviour – driving ambition, burning pride, a large amount of money, the love of a woman or a chronic case of piles. But they share a common trait: a total disregard for the consequences....

Defusing a Terrorist Bomb

Your big chance to go from idiot to hero...

You wipe a bead of sweat off your forehead, glance quickly at the watching crowd, safely placed miles away, and turn back to the matter in hand. Tick, tick, tick... you grip the cutters and take a deep breath, red or blue? Blue! Tick, tick, tick... No, no, red! That's the point when your mum usually wakes you...

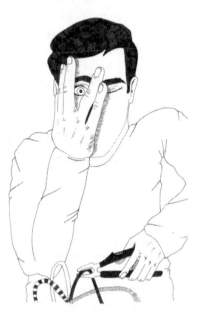

But what if you really came across a terrorist bomb – have you got the *cojones* to make it safe? Ideally you'll have intricate knowledge of chemistry (remember those lessons with Bunsen burners and cobalt chloride?), considerable bomb disposal experience and a steady hand – still, you're good at video games and have seen them defused in the movies enough times, so why not?

Take a look at the device – it will have three components: explosives, timer and detonator. Your job is simply to disconnect these elements – without blowing yourself to kingdom come. There's no point looking for sticks of gelignite, red wires and a digital alarm clock – modern terrorists refuse to play the game and now use a host of materials from liquid explosives to mobile phones. Good luck with that.

Dangerous Idiot Odds
Arrest 4
Injury 4
Death 4

Surgery Without Anaesthetic

Why the blood-curdling scream? The idiot with a low-pain threshold has just gone under the knife...

"Just a little prick," they always say. But what would they say if you declined the imminent injection or even the proffered gas mask? Could your ingrowing toenail, veruca removal or even open-heart surgery be much more painful than removing a splinter with a needle or carving your girlfriend's initials in your arm? In a word: yes.

The first successful operation under anaesthetic was carried out in 1847 and since then only those experimenting with hypnosis or undergoing operations in emergency situations have suffered non-anaesthetized surgery. But for the dangerous idiot there are no boundaries. Screens please, nurse...

If you are looking for some reading material in the waiting room, have a look at some pre-1847 surgeons' reports. Witnessing one operation was enough to put a young Charles Darwin off medicine as a career, while other doctors recall being haunted for life by the screams and cries of pain. Or read the excruciating recollections of victims of Anaesthetic Awareness, the one in 700 people who wake up during surgery.

There is one thing that might help. A 1999 study by the Yale School of Medicine suggested that listening to music might not only block out the sounds of flesh cutting and bone sawing but may also reduce the blood flow. So get your ipod ready – we suggest 'The First Cut is Deepest', 'Everybody Hurts' or 'We've Gotta Get Out of this Place'.

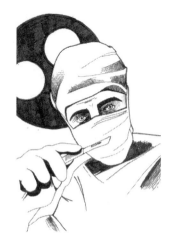

Dangerous Idiot Odds
Arrest – 0 stars
Injury – 4 stars
Death – 2 stars

It'll take more than a stiff drink to prepare yourself for this one!

Fighting a Crocodile

He's 20 ft (6 m) long, weighs over a ton, but has just picked on the wrong guy...

OK, so the form book is not on your side. The crocodile is aggressive, quick, incredibly strong, can kill in a few seconds and despatches around 3,000 people a year. You are dim-witted, slow and hide in the toilet when it all goes off in the pub. But there are a few tips and tricks that might help to balance the bout...

First, know your enemy. Crocodiles are most aggressive in the mating system; they can hide in only 1 ft (30 cm) of water and like to perform a "death roll", biting, gripping and rapidly spinning to weaken their prey. Oh, and they have the strongest biting force of any animal alive – exceeding 5,000 psi.

However, they do lack stamina – put up a fight and you have a chance – and if you approach them from behind you might just surprise them. Get your bodyweight on the croc's back and legs over their hind feet but watch that whipping tail. Use both hands to force the neck down and the crocodile's jaws should close; grip them to keep them shut (they have strong muscles for closing jaws but weak ones for opening).

Now slide your legs down the body until they are able to stop the tail moving. Grip tightly and hold this position. Three seconds should be enough for you to be declared the winner...

Dangerous Idiot Odds
Arrest 1
Injury 5
Death 3

Alternatively, get your girlfriend to shout "leave him babe,
he's not worth it" and walk away with dignity...

Eyeball Tattoo

Definitely not one for the squeamish...

Pain is subjective. One man's "excruciating" is another's "mild discomfort". However, I think we can agree that an injection in the eyeball is a pretty unbearable idea. Yet, eyeball tattoos are a must in the real body-adorning circles.

Originating, as many tattoo traditions have, in prisons – eye tattoos have become a craze in many US penitentiaries. Well, you'd want to look your best for slopping out time wouldn't you? Oklahoma prisons had such a rush on eye jobs that in 2009 the state passed a law banning them – and it's a pretty tough crime to conceal!

There isn't exactly room for a heart with "mum" written across it or an anchor, so tatooees settle for colouring in the whites of the eyes. The method of choice is to use a syringe to pierce the eye and inject a pigment, drop by drop. Unfortunately it takes at least 40 injections to complete the job – apparently it feels like having hot ice-picks jabbed in your eyes, over and over again.

Safe? Of course not. Ophthalmologists claim it can lead to infection, perforation, haemorrhages or even blindness and those who have had it done say it feels like there's something permanently stuck in their eye. Still, it looks pretty – or pretty scary!

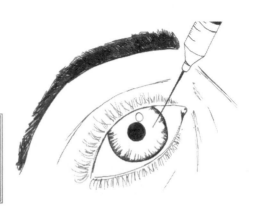

```
Dangerous Idiot Odds
Arrest 4
Injury 4
Death 1
```

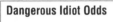

Well that's one in the eye for the body modifiers…

Vacuum-Packed Spiderman

Is it a superhero? Is it a spider? No. It's a complete idiot...

Spiderman was always the coolest of the superheroes – something about the way he glided up those walls. A bite from a radioactive spider gave Peter Parker the power of vertical ascendancy and suddenly he was transformed from an awkward teenager to a cool superhero. If only, you say, we could find something to change you from a dangerous idiot to a dangerous idiot stuck half way up a wall...

Well, with a simple home-made wall -limbing system made from a couple of old vacuum cleaners, you can impress your mates by shimmering up any wall. Scientist Jem Stansfield proved it was possible, he fixed two 1,500 watt vacuum cleaners to a board and attached "gloves" – plywood pads the size of a small tea tray with a rubber seal – to the tubes. Hoisting the board, rucksack style onto his back, the 12-stone (76 kg) scientist managed to walk 120 ft (36m) up the side of the building.

As each glove could hold his whole weight, he could afford to change hands in order to scale the wall. OK, he did have the luxury of a safety harness, but that doesn't seem that essential – you need some risk and being three stories high held up by a couple of budget supermarket cleaners seems more than enough comfort for the average idiot...

Dangerous Idiot Odds
Arrest 2
Injury 4
Death 2

If you also had "Spidersense" – the superhero's innate sense of danger – you'd throw this book away now

Wheel Well Stowaway

No films, flight attendants or small packets of nuts...

Those darn terrorists have really ruined the fun for everyone. There was a time when any idiot on a free death trip could jump into the wheel well and enjoy a funeral in a far off country. Nowadays, airport security is so strict you're lucky to get out of duty-free without a strip search. But if an intrepid adventurer manages to climb into the wheel pit of a 747, what are his chances of getting out alive?

Well, let's just say it's not the safest of seats on the plane. While the landing gears are up he could be swept away by the wind and, as the gears retract, there's an equal chance of being crushed. Get through that and it's just a matter of not being scorched by the heat of the engines as the plane gains altitude and then not contracting hypothermia as temperatures plunge to -76°F (-60°c), suffocating due to a lack of oxygen in the unpressurized well or falling out as the plane prepares for take-off. Oh – did I forget to mention nitrogen gas embolism and decompression sickness?

But don't be downhearted. Since 1947 there have been 74 known airplane stowaway attempts worldwide and 14 of those have survived (who knows how many have scampered away on landing) – even after altitudes of over 35,000 ft (11 km). Generally under 35, they appear to be have been able to hibernate temporarily and resuscitate themselves on descent. Maybe you could practice sleeping in the fridge?

Dangerous Idiot Odds
Arrest 5
Injury 4
Death 5

Aren't you taking no-frills air travel just a little too far?

Set a Groin-Kicking Record

So you never made the football team, flunked your exams, get beaten at pool by the blind bloke in the pub – here's something that might just put you at the top of the pile...

Being kicked square in the groin is a pretty unforgettable experience – you feel enveloped by a feeling of intense pain up and down your body, followed by breathlessness, dizziness and nausea until it just becomes a desperate ache for days on end. Sound like something you could do as a day job?

Kirby Roy set a world record by being kicked where it hurts most by American Gladiator and MMA fighter Justice Smith, who delivered a 22mph (35 kph) blow with 1,100lbs (500 kg) of force, while an Indian, Bibhuti Bhushan Nayak, had three 41lbs (19 kg) blocks placed on his groin before being smashed with a sledgehammer. He also holds the record for getting the most kicks to the groin, a mighty 43.

Of course (as the song says) you want fame and here's where you start paying. Strikes at the family jewels can cause death, scrotum tear and the loss of testosterone and sperm-making capabilities. But there is good news; practice hard and you will also produce less Substance P, a tissue extract that transmits pain – so every kick you receive should be less painful than the last...

Dangerous Idiot Odds
Arrest 0
Injury 4
Death 1

Ouch!

Fight a Giant Squid

Who are you calling a cephalopoda?

Might you be attacked by a giant squid? It happened in the *Lord of the Rings*; it was the basis of the *Jaws*' author Peter Benchley's book and film *The Beast* and, most memorably, it happened to James Bond at the climax of *Dr No*, so it's worth being prepared.

Giant squid are thought to grow up to 66 ft (20 m) from the fin to the tip of the longest tentacle. They have five pairs of tentacles, one set being the gripping tentacles complete with claws around the suckers; a beak-like mouth strong enough to cut through steel cable; and a radula (a tongue with small, file-like teeth) that could rip you to shreds. These rock-hard beasts regularly spar with sperm whales, often taking them down after an extensive bout. Yep, giant squid *own* the ocean.

If you are going to take one on you'll need to take a leaf out of 007's book and get beyond the tentacles to the body. The squid has 18 in (45 cm) diameter eyes, so you've got a big target. Pierce, gouge or rip and you'll find the sly scrapper spurting out his famous black ink. In the ensuing confusion, you'll be grateful for those years spent practising tying knots in the dark , as you incapacitate each pair of tentacles in turn.

Now swim for all your worth – but keep a look out for the the Colossal Squid. Bigger and more aggressive, the Giant Squid's cousin might just be a fight to far...

Dangerous Idiot Odds
Arrest 3
Injury 4
Death 4

It's calamari and chips all round guys!

Car Surfing

Who needs an ocean to catch the big one?

Cowabunga! Looking not only for an adrenaline rush but to raise the hackles of concerned citizens everywhere? Just remember, spill on this one and it's not a gentle drop to the Pacific and a sore ego but a ditch by the side of a B-road, broken you-name-it and severe concussion.

Inspired partly by the 1985 film *Teen Wolf*, in which Michael J Fox indulged in a little car surfing , this stunt involves simply climbing onto the roof, bonnet or boot of a moving car and clinging on for dear life as the driver shifts through the gears.

Beginners lie spread-eagled on the roof desperately clinging to the sides, windows or roof bars, but experienced surfers have been known to stand up and "shoot the breeze." Mad? You betcha! Anything over around 20mph (32 kph) and your grip is going to be severely tested.

Still not a big enough thrill for you? The California craze of Ghost Riding is even more scary. With your car stereo on at full blast (best replace the Britney CD with something hardcore though), you put the car in gear – or even jam the accelerator, then get out and "bust a move" on your own bonnet. So far, eight deaths and counting...

Dangerous Idiot Odds
Arrest 5
Injury 5
Death 3

Oh Well! That's the Ford Focus written off…

Fugu and Chips

"And our special today is to die for..."

Next time your mate tries to impress you by ordering the hottest vindaloo on the menu, challenge him to eat something really risky: puffer fish – also known as blowfish, sea squab or, in Japan, fugu, where it is a real delicacy, but one often eaten with trepidation.

The body of a puffer fish contains a tetrodotoxin, a poison 1,200 times more deadly than cyanide. Cooking does not destroy the toxins and there is no known antidote. One puffer fish contains enough poison – in its liver, intestines and skin – to kill 30 people

In many countries it is illegal to cook the fish and, in Japan, chefs require a special licence to prepare the fish and undergo an exam (with only a 25 percent pass rate), where they must prepare and then eat a meal of puffer fish. Despite this, some 100–200 people still suffer from tetrodotoxin poisoning every year. Approximately half of these cases result in death.

A bite-size piece of puffer fish will be enough to poison a man within minutes. First you feel a tingling of the mouth, then vomiting, dizziness and, eventually, paralysis. Many victims remain alive for a while but paralysed in a zombie-type state, so don't dismiss it as just too much lager. However, there is some good news, if you survive the first 24 hours, the chances are you'll live.

Dangerous Idiot Odds	
Arrest	3
Injury	3
Death	3

It's the fish dish that bites back

Fire Breathing

Feeling a little hot under the collar? Let it out the dangerous way...

Clowns? Yeah great. Mime? Yawn. Jugglers? Give us a break. But everyone loves the human dragons – they're dangerous, cool and slightly out-of-control in a freaky, hippy way. If you are looking to join them, the good news is that the fire-breathing technique is pretty simple; the bad news is that if it goes wrong, it goes very, very wrong...

All you have to do is "spit" a fine mist of highly flammable liquid over a flame. You can practice in the bathroom with water – take a mouthful, purse your lips as if you are blowing a trumpet and spay. Your ultimate success will depend on how fine you can make the vapour.

Next you can start practising with paraffin – the only safe fuel to use. Have a glass of milk first, because if you swallow any paraffin it'll keep the severe diarrhoea down to a few days. When you're ready to light your breath, it's probably time to move your practice sessions to the car park of the local A & E.

Things can now go either one of two ways. You could really turn on the style: blowing immense fireballs, firing "farts" back between your legs and bouncing fire off the ground or you could be signing up for the biggest burden on the NHS. A sudden gust of wind might be enough to land you with severe burns though stomach ulcers, poisoning and dental problems could all be on their way.

Dangerous Idiot Odds	
Arrest	4
Injury	5
Death	1

Whatever, remember to film it – everyone will enjoy you being flambéd on Youtube...

Part Seven

Welcome to the Freak Show

Are these people human? The great public fascination with extraordinary, awe-inspiring feats has never really diminished. What once drew queues at 19th century fairgrounds now draws thousands of hits on Youtube. But where do these idiot heroes come from...?

Become a Human Blockhead

One of the great freak show acts and it's no trick ...

The Human Blockhead (invented by Coney Island sideshow performer Melvin Burkhart), is the name of the brilliant stunt where the performer hammers a nail into his skull. Easy, you're thinking – that's a collapsible nail or some sleight of hand. No way! Get the tool kit out, you're really going to have to bang a nail into your head...

The act utilizes the space between bones in the human skull – specifically the nasal cavity, a large air-filled space above and behind the nose. The size of the cavity varies from person to person but should be large enough for a 6 in (15 cm) nail.

The cavity is accessible through the nostrils – your job is to just practise finding it with a sharp metal object, which should be fun. As mucous membranes line all of the surfaces, there should be plenty of lubrication, but expect a fair few nosebleeds along the way. Once you've mastered the technique, the showman in you can take over, bringing out the electric drill, sledgehammer, pneumatic drill...

Your biggest obstacle will be overcoming the sneeze reflex. If you're a big sneezer you could find the nail diverting into any number of vital organs around your skull. It is possible to fight the sneeze, but you'll be teaching your body to let in all kinds of harmful foreign objects (as well as nails) and you could well become a virus magnet.

Dangerous Idiot Odds
Arrest 0
Injury 4
Death 1

Next time your mum tells you not to pick your nose, show her this one...

Blow Up a Hot-Water Bottle

Have you got the puff for the ultimate party trick?

Do you have trouble blowing up those long balloons you get in party bags? If so, skip this page, you're never going to have enough puff to inflate a hot-water bottle. But if you think you have the required lung power, this is a super-impressive stunt with more than a hint of serious danger.

The thickness and strength of the rubber hot-water bottle initially make it almost impossible to inflate by mouth to any visible degree. But by practising, building up your facial muscles and lung capacity and by stretching the rubber as you do a party balloon, you might reach the point where you can inflate the bottle to a diameter of around 3ft (90 cm) and on to bursting point.

For a party trick the risks are pretty high. You'll be inflating the water bottles to more than 170 lbs (77kg) per sq in (6sq cm), that's twice the pressure of a truck tyre and the kind of force that can collapse a lung if the air rushed back at you. Then, when it explodes, it will whip rubber back against your face, causing serious welts and possible blindness. That's why experienced blowers use a ski mask and goggles.

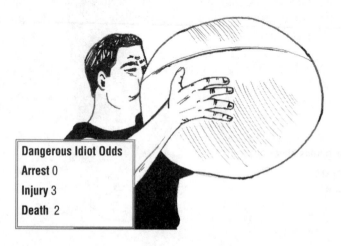

Dangerous Idiot Odds
Arrest 0
Injury 3
Death 2

Now make a giraffe out of it

Eating a Lightbulb

Why did the Dangerous Idiot eat a lightbulb? Because he wanted a light snack!

Why did the Dangerous Idiot really eat a light bulb? Because he's an attention-seeker subverting his fears for subconscious gratification. Light-bulb eating is standard fare in the circus sideshow canteen but elsewhere it is rarely performed outside of drunken student parties – for a very good reason.

Before you start munching keep in mind that the key to the stunt is to grind the glass into the smallest possible pieces. They will pass through your intestines without perforating any major organs and you might even survive the ordeal. Use your molars (teeth at the back) to chew the glass and keep your tongue well out of the way.

In preparation for the meal, you should have given your digestive system a diet of high-fibre foods to keep foods moving through the system. But, you probably won't have bothered, so have a banana and some yoghurt to ease the path of the glass and hope for the best.

Discard the metal socket (what kind of fool would eat that?) and tuck in. Take your time, but don't bore your audience – a few minutes for a 60 watt bulb should do the trick. Now wait, the worst is still to come, for when they say "there's a light at the end of tunnel" it's not always good news...

Dangerous Idiot Odds
Arrest 0
Injury 4
Death 2

If you're having trouble try it with a little ketchup...

Head Butting a Breeze Block

For black belts, Tenth Dans and true idiots it's the ultimate martial art challenge...

It's tough, dramatic and not a little spiritual – achieve this feat and you'll be reaching the heights of real dangerous idiocy. Once the preserve of shaolin monks, the head butting of solid materials is now open to anyone with the inclination and the necessary breeze block.

Utilizing the weight of the head – about 11 lbs (5kg) which is the same as a light bowling ball – and the power of the body you could provide enough impact to shatter the concrete, but you'll need to get your technique right. You are going to throw your head forward and down concentrating the strike on the toughest part of your skull, the area 1 in (2.5 cm) above your eyebrow.

Clenching your teeth and keeping your mouth shut, bring the movement up from your middle back through your neck muscles to swing your head, dipping your knees just before impact. Your aim is to shock the block, causing it to fracture and then drive on through, but to do this you are going to have to get your head moving through the air at over 50 ft (15 m) a second.

Now the metaphysical bit. You have to believe. This feat requires not only strength on the outer head, but inside as well. Any hesitation and doubt and you'll end up with a large gash across your forehead – come to think of it, that's probably what is going to happen anyway.

Dangerous Idiot Odds
Arrest 0
Injury 5
Death 2

Don't tell me – you need this one like a hole in the head?

Sword Swallowing

A great traditional sideshow act that is fantastically dangerous and a real audience stunner.

Many observers believe sword swallowing to be a trick, after all, what idiot would slide a real sword down their gullet? However, there is no trick or illusion, just a well practised stunt that has an enormous risk of going completely Pete Tong and lacerating any number of major organs.

When you pass a sword through your throat down the oesophagus and into the stomach, it is following the same path that any food would take, along the gastrointestinal (GI) tract. The GI tract is the body's very own sheath and, if it weren't for its natural curvature, a not easily accessible stomach and the gag reflex, you might think it was designed for sword swallowing.

Begin by leaning your head back and extending your neck as far as possible. Lubricate the sword with saliva and pass it through the mouth and past the pharynx. Use the sword, very gently, to straighten the flexible oesophagus and nudge organs out of the way as it descends, then bring your oesophagus and stomach in line (a few pints of water can help orientate the stomach).

What can possibly go wrong? OK. If you can get past the gag reflex without constantly vomiting, any slight error can pierce your windpipe, lungs or heart – at the very least you will almost certainly get "sword throat" and be unable to eat for days.

Dangerous Idiot Odds
Arrest 1
Injury 5
Death 2

I'd recommend a little ice cream for dessert…

Stub a Cigarette Out on Your Tongue

Learn this trick and you'll never want for an ashtray.

These days it's hard being a smoker – you're made to feel like a pariah and there's never anywhere to stub out your butt. But who could resist someone cool enough to stub out his lighted ciggie on his own tongue?

First of all, practice this when you are alone and make sure you get it right. The whole point of the stunt is that you are going to look cool. That's not going to happen if you spend five minutes hopping around the room and dipping your tongue into a glass of iced water.

Make sure you mouth is well lubricated before stubbing – hopefully you are going to keep the cigarette right in the centre of your tongue but it's not worth taking any chances. Swill an icy drink around your mouth, but most of all make sure there is plenty of saliva and liquid on your tongue. Now take your lighted cigarette and push it sharply and firmly into the centre of your tongue, twisting it as you do so. You should practice on an ashtray to ensure you are able to extinguish the cigarette in one thrust.

Don't flinch no matter how much it hurts – meditate, screw your toes into the soles of your feet or just hold the pain until you get outside – the more nonchalant you are, the more effective the performance.

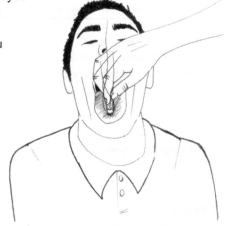

Dangerous Idiot Odds	
Arrest	0
Injury	4
Death	0

If you're lucky you'll have the pick of companions for the rest of the party, if not you could have a mouth full of ash and third-degree burns

Scorpion vs Butt

Pointless, stupid, dangerous and rude – it's got it all!

It's the ultimate college dare – requiring a fair bit of Dutch courage, the ubiquitous lowering of the trousers and a real idiot willing to go through intense pain in order that everyone else (and thousands online) can have a good laugh.

You – with some assistance – are about to hold a scorpion between your naked butt cheeks for a count of ten. There are about 1,400 species of scorpion and only 25 of these have venom potent enough to kill a human. All you have to do is make sure you don't use one these for your dare. The Emperor Scorpion might be a good choice – it looks a fiercesome dude but is one of the more docile of the species.

While you are removing your trousers and underwear and taking up a suitable position, your assistant should take hold of the scorpion, gently grabbing its tail with a pair of tweezers. They should try not to alarm the scorpion (although how alarmed would you feel if you were about to be slotted into someone's bum-crack?) and gently place the creature in the required crevice.

It's OK. After the initial agony – like an electric jolt of 1,000 volts – and a general numbing of the body, the pain will gradually subside. You'll need an ice compress on it for a few hours and you won't sit down for a few days. But you'll have a great cellphone clip to send to your mates.

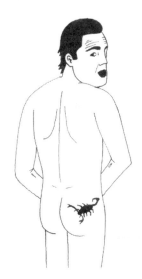

Dangerous Idiot Odds
Arrest 2
Injury 5
Death 1

The dare with a sting in a tail

Eye Popping

So dangerous, you could have someone's eye out – yours!

You know how it is, you're bored, there's nothing on TV and there's nearly an hour until tea. You need something quick and exciting to amuse you. Now's the time to consider eye popping – taking your eyeball out of its socket – a hobby more dangerous than Monopoly but usually easier to tidy away.

Some people find the trick easier than others. It all depends on your globes. If you are lucky you can pop them both by closing your mouth and nose and exhaling with as much force as you can. Others need a little fiddling and pushing, a bit like taking your contact lenses out, while a few of you might end up losing your sight either temporarily or permanently.

The effect though is quite stunning. You'll achieve, at worst, a fantastic comic-book look with huge bug eyes but if you can get the eyeball to hang by the optic nerve and rest on top of your cheek , it will seriously freak out anyone who is watching.

Getting the eyeballs back in the socket isn't quite so easy. You'll need to hold back the lashes and poke the eyeball (touching only the less sensitive white part) gently back into the socket. It's probably best to let a professional (doctor or freakshow entertainer) do it for you.

Within a few days you will hopefully be seeing reasonably well and, after a week or two, won't even need to wear your shades around the house.

Dangerous Idiot Odds
Arrest 0
Injury 4
Death 1

Have you got an eye for the ladies?

Juggling Chainsaws

Been wondering what to do with all those old chainsaws?

Juggling is a delicate skill of timing, technique and co-ordination. So how come it's down there with mime as one of the most tedious of circus skills? Because there's no danger. Introduce the possibility of lopping off one of your limbs in mid-air and the whole thing becomes a whole lot more palatable.

Jugglers tell us that once you learn how to juggle a set of balls, discs or clubs you can tackle anything. If you've never juggled anything – why not start with chainsaws, you've nothing to lose but your hands. Take one chainsaw firmly by the handle and practise throwing it with your right hand so it spins once in the air before catching it in your left. Once you have mastered that try throwing with the left and catching with your right hand. OK your toes are going to get pretty hammered, but get used to catching with soft hands, letting the handle implant itself in your palm.

Now move on to throwing one, catching it and moving it over to the other hand. Get this sorted and you've cracked it – one in the air and one being thrown from hand to hand. Confident? Then try this. Start with two in your left and one in the right. Toss with the right, pass with the left. Toss the new one under the arc of the first and get into the rhythm – throw, pass, throw, catch, pass...

Now start the vicious machines and see if you still fancy doing it?

Dangerous Idiot Odds
Arrest 1
Injury 4
Death 2

"The Texas Chainsaw Juggling Massacre – take 32!"

Human Cannonball

The ideal pursuit for a man of your calibre...

No doubt you will share my disappointment on discovering that the circus human cannonball does not use anything like gunpowder to fire its shot, but relies on compressed air or a catapult mechanism (much like the human trebuchet on page 81). The smoke and explosion are merely to entertain. This is not to say there haven't been numerous injuries and even fatalities, but the circus act lacks the frisson required to make it truly dangerous and idiotic.

So why not be fired like a true cannonball. You'll need a friend who has no fear of prosecution for manslaughter and a working cannon big enough for a person to fit tightly. For a 32in (81 cm) diameter cannon, you'll need to make a silver foil parcel with about 8lbs (4 kg) of black gunpowder and push it down the barrel until it is packed tightly at the firing end. Now insert a fuse into the parcel – making sure it's long enough to give enough time for your mate to get away.

Now you are ready to be fired. Dress accordingly, something aerodynamic maybe, but bright enough to help those picking up the pieces afterwards. Crawl down the barrel getting as close to the powder as possible, get your mate to point the cannon at the local funeral directors and give the instruction to fire...

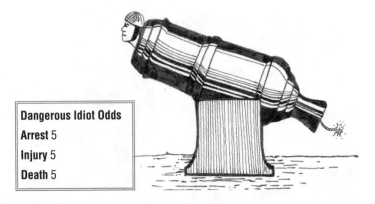

Dangerous Idiot Odds
Arrest 5
Injury 5
Death 5

Everyone's got a talent… could this be yours?

Knife Throwing

All the fun of the fair in a display of skill, showmanship and possible murder....

The drums roll and pause. The crowd squeals in anticipation as you take up the knives. You make eye contact with your target girl, draw back your first knife and send it turning through the air. It seems an eternity but eventually it lands – a moment of horror, a single scream from the audience and a look of desperate pleading from the beautiful assistant as she slumps to a bloody puddle on the floor. B*ll*cks you think – I knew I should have practised...

Practise really is the key to this art – learning to grip the knife by the tip, between the thumb and forefinger; perfecting a flick throw that sends it on at least two rotations across a distance of 15-30 ft (5-10 m) and, most importantly, throwing it enough times to be confident of hitting the exact spot you are aiming at, every time. Only then can you try and find an assistant – beautiful or otherwise – mad enough to risk her life just for you to show off.

Your blades should be landing so close you almost graze the target's skin. Of course, the true showman will not be rest here – try the wheel of death where you impale her on a large, circular spinning board; place a paper cover in front of your target or learn to throw while blindfolded. Until your beautiful assistant decides that a boring office job looks quite appealing after all...

Dangerous Idiot Odds
Arrest 3
Injury 2
Death 0

At last! A dangerous pursuit where you're not the one who's going to get hurt

Bed of Nails

Your chance to lie down on the job.

Stripping to the waist, harnessing your inner strength, preparing for intense pain, you grimace and lie back on the bed of 1,000 sharp nails, each a sharp point capable of piercing the skin. Unbearable agony? A supreme test of endurance? Well, no. You'll barely suffer a scratch actually. As any schoolboy know...

A bed of nails has hundreds of nails and can actually support the weight of your body. Your body doesn't exert enough pressure on any one nail for it to puncture the skin. As long as all the nails are the same height, you should be able to pull of the stunt completely unhurt. Just be careful how you get on and off the bed.

So what can we do to make it a little more thrilling? Let's see how much you can take. Place a piece of plywood over the top of your body. Still no pain? Place a concrete block on top of the plywood. You could feel a little uncomfortable now but dangerous? Pah! OK, get serious. Get a friend to take a sledge hammer and bring it down heavily on the concrete block. OK. It might be starting to hurt a little now but you're ready for the climax of the demonstration. Two friends, carefully distributing their weight, can climb onto the smashed block.

If you've got your physics right, you should be fine. If not, there will be blood!

Dangerous Idiot Odds
Arrest 0
Injury 3
Death 0

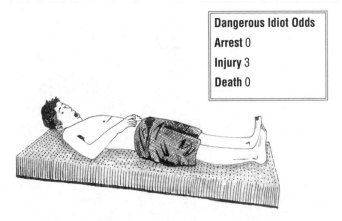

Are you a fakir or a faker?

Part Eight
Off the Scale

Now it seems there's nowhere left to go... You've tried every half-baked cock-a-nanny idea that could get you arrested, concussed, bone-busted and flat-lined and yet the adrenaline trickles and the pulse beats out it's funereal pace. It's time to go off the scale...

DIY Trepanation

Tense, nervous, headache?
Try drilling a hole into your brain...

Perhaps, like Prince Charles, you appreciate the alternative medicines – a little acupuncture, some essential oils, a whisky and lemon. If so, you might see the healing benefits of trepanation, a surgical method used in ancient times to treat virtually every ailment imaginable – and effective on absolutely none.

Trepanation is the practice of boring a hole in the skull to... Well, it's not really clear. Some say it releases the pressure, lets the brain breathe or lets the evil spirits escape – while modern hippy talk insists it increases the flow of blood to the brain returning you to a child-like, simple outlook on life. For your simple needs it's enough to know it's ridiculous and could well kill you.

To perform self-trepanation at home, take a sharp knife and cut a cross as deep as you can about 2 in (5cm) above your left eye. Now, using an electric drill with a bit the size of a five pence (or one cent) coin, drill down through the cross until you pierce the skull. The idea is to drill a "third eye" also called "the eye of the mind" (see what we're dealing with here?).

The skin should eventually grow over the wound but the hole should be big enough so that the bone will not mend. If you've successfully avoided infection, meningitis or brain damage you should be as right as rain in six months or so...

Dangerous Idiot Odds
Arrest 5
Injury 5
Death 5

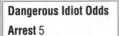

Be honest, you need this treatment like you need a hole in the head

Crossing US19 on Crutches

Why did the idiot cross the road?

Picture the scene – after a recent sporting injury (possibly after one of the ideas in this book) has left you on crutches, you have taken a break in Pasco County, Florida. One balmy early evening you decide to cross US Highway 19 to get to Wal-Mart for some aspirin. Stop right there! You are about to attempt one of the most dangerous stunts in this book. Before you take another hop, read on and assess your chances of survival.

Recent surveys of crashes, injuries and fatalities have led to this stretch of road being declared the most dangerous in America. Trucks thunder down the six-lane highway, a major thoroughfare running all the way between Lake Erie and the Gulf of Mexico. On the Pasco County stretch it has claimed the lives of over 100 pedestrians in the last five years.

"But I'm pretty nippy on these things," you argue – still reckoning you can get across and back in the ad break in *Glee*. Oh yeah? You're talking 130 ft (40 m)each way at a speed of around 2 ft (0.6 m) per second. That's over a minute in which to avoid vehicles often speeding at more than 100mph (160 kph)– in the dark! Make the 10ft (3m) wide central reservation and your heart will be in your mouth.

Take my advice and try any of the other stunts in the book before this one (OK, with the exception of the last one – but don't look yet) .

Dangerous Idiot Odds	
Arrest	1
Injury	5
Death	5

Look right, look left…aaaaaaahhh!

Over Niagara Falls in a Barrel

A legendary challenge for any budding daredevil...

Ever since 63-year-old schoolteacher, Annie Edson Taylor, climbed in a barrel with her cat, a pillow and an anvil (for ballast) in 1901, pitched herself over Niagara Falls and survived, the feat has attracted the mad and desperate. Since Annie, 14 others have taken the plunge in barrels or other devices. Of those, 10 have survived.

And its allure remains – despite the idea of falling 170 ft (51 m) at 75mph (120 kph); being battered inside the barrel by the crushing flow of 600,000 gallons (2,730, 000 l) of water per second; hitting the huge jutting rocks at the base of the falls, then undergoing another 180 ft (55 m) drop to the Maids of the Mist pool; and, if you survive, you'll face a fine of $10,000 for "stunting without a license".

To come out dripping but smiling you'll need more than an old beer barrel from your local (well Bobby Leach managed that in 1911 but he did break his jaw and both kneecaps). Successful attempts have been made using steel balls reinforced with rubber, Greek pickle barrels strengthened by fibreglass and a barrel padded with the material that the military uses to pack nuclear warheads.

Dangerous Idiot Odds
Arrest 5
Injury 5
Death 5

And you thought the top board at the local pool was a little high

Russian Roulette

Feeling lucky, punk? Because you're about to play for the biggest stakes of all – your life.

Originating in a game played by mad or suicidal 19th century Russian soldiers, this cheery, rainy-day pastime was made popular by the edge-of-the-seat scene in the movie *The Deerhunter*. The rules are simple: players sit in a circle, the first to play puts one bullet into a six-chamber revolver, spins the cylinder, puts the gun to his head and pulls the trigger. If he survives, he passes the gun to the player on his left who takes a turn – and so on until the agreed number of players lie motionless in a pool of blood.

On the plus side you experience a fantastic adrenaline rush and still have a five-in-six chance of survival. The downside is that if you do happen to survive, you'll have some pretty messy cleaning up to do. What? This still isn't enough of an idiot trip for you? How about not re-spinning after each shot? This brings down the odds significantly; the second player has a one-in-five chance of eating lead, the third one-in-four, etc, until, if it gets as far as a sixth turn, someone will have to get his (metaphysical) coat.

Note: if you sit more on the "idiot" than the "dangerous" side of the fence, try playing "The Beerhunter". Madly shake one can of a six-pack of beer, place it randomly back in the pack and take turns to open a can with the opening facing your nose.

Dangerous Idiot Odds	
Arrest	5
Injury	1
Death	3

There's no skill, no chance of cheating but it's a lot more riveting than Cluedo...

Crocodile Bungee

Just don't lose your head over this great idea...

As dangerous activities go, bungee jumping isn't really that challenging. A few seconds plunging freefall through the air and a humiliating dangling wait for the gormless stoner to get round to helping you out of the harness. So you try to max up the thrills – do a 300 ft (90 m) jump, re-enact James Bond's *Goldeneye* jump off Verzasca Dam in Switzerland, or head for the highest one of all: the 765 ft (233 m) high Macau Tower in China. But there's still no real chance of injury short of a pulled muscle or two.

Around 2005, a viral video showed a camcorder-style clip of an Australian bungee jumper "Big Doug" plunging down and dipping into a river only to be snapped at by a waiting crocodile and emerge without a head. It turned out that the clip was part of a beer advert and the crocodile had been added with special effects wizardry.

But why waste a good idea? The Nile crocodile would be your best bet – no stranger to a little man-eating, it is thought to devour between 200 and 1,000 humans a year. It will attack anything that crosses its path and has lightning quick reactions. Try jumping above the Rufiji River in Tanzania, home to some of the biggest crocs in the world, and you could have a queue of idiots just waiting to part with their money – and their heads...

Dangerous Idiot Odds
Arrest 0
Injury 4
Death 3

At last some real fear at the end of the elastic...

Perform Hara Kiri

We've left the most dangerous to last...

There are some humiliations that just can't be tolerated: your team goes out of the cup to a part-time team of milkmen and roofers, your girlfriend dumps you for the weedy nerd next door and, your mum turns up on *Snog, Marry, Avoid*. Years ago, the Japanese came up with the perfect solution – a ritual suicide that restores honour and dignity to the humbled...

The words *hara kiri* mean "stomach cutting", and this is literally what you have to do. In a kneeling position, take your sword and plunge it into the left side of your abdomen then swiftly move it across to the right. Now, if you can, insert the knife again and cut down from your chest through your belly. If you have done it properly your guts will spill neatly onto your lap. Oh, one more thing: try to pretend it doesn't hurt – any screaming lowers the kudos you get from your dramatic exit.

Finally it's your mate's turn – if he hasn't fainted. He must perform *dakikubi*, beheading you in one sweep of the sword except he needs to leave a small band of skin so your head is still, just, connected to your body.

The one great thing about this dangerous pursuit is that you won't be the one left to clean up...

Dangerous Idiot Odds
Arrest 0
Injury 4
Death 5

Do this before the rest of the challenges in the book and you're even more stupid than I thought!